IN CONFLICT

Also by Yvonne Latty

*We Were There: Voices of African American Veterans,
from World War II to the War in Iraq*

IN CONFLICT

Iraq War Veterans
Speak Out on Duty, Loss,
and the Fight to Stay Alive

* * *

YVONNE LATTY

Foreword by
Former U.S. Senator MAX CLELAND

PoliPointPress

In Conflict: Iraq War Veterans Speak Out on Duty, Loss,
and the Fight to Stay Alive
by Yvonne Latty

Copyright © 2006 Yvonne Latty.

This edition published in 2006 in the United States of America by
PoliPointPress, P.O. Box 3008, Sausalito, CA 94966.
www.PoliPointPress.org

Production management: Michael Bass Associates
Book design: Linda M. Robertson, LMR Designs

Library of Congress Cataloging-in-Publication Data

Latty, Yvonne
In Conflict: Iraq War Veterans Speak Out on Duty, Loss, and the Fight
to Stay Alive/Yvonne Latty; foreword by Max Cleland
ISBN: 0-9760621-4-3

Library of Congress Control Number: 2005910606

Printed in the United States of America
March 2006

Published by:
PoliPointPress, LLC
P.O. Box 3008
Sausalito, CA 94966-3008
(415) 339-4100
www.PoliPointPress.org

Distributed by Publishers Group West

To my two daughters, Nola and Margo,
who make me want to fight hard to make
this world a better place filled with
compassion, understanding, and peace.

Contents

CONTENTS

FOREWORD

Former U.S. Senator MAX CLELAND

Marcus Childs, a distinguished columnist for the *Washington Post*, once wrote about war, "Only a few do the fighting and the dying."

In terms of the American military, that statement has never been truer than it is today. We have the smallest army as a nation we've had since before World War II. It is all volunteer. The active force, even the National Guard and reserves, have become an American Foreign Legion deployed like a 911 force all over the world. Young Americans have been sent to hot spots around the globe in recent years to fight and to die in Panama, Somalia, Bosnia, Kosovo, and now Iraq and Afghanistan. The wisdom of their being sent to these wars is debatable. The courage of their performance is not.

Most of us have an eerie detachment from the lives of these young warriors. We see their experiences thorough the prism of the media babble and the political tug-of-war which their deployment ultimately brings. But, we are still armchair generals. We can change the channel.

They cannot.

It takes a real journalist and artist along the lines of the legendary Ernie Pyle to make their lives real to us, to have us participate in their suffering. Such an author is Yvonne Latty. But, more than Ernie Pyle, she lets these warriors speak for themselves. As much as possible, she gets out of the way and lets them tell their stories.

Their tales of war and its impact on them are breathtaking. They rivet us in our seats, and they hit us in the gut. We are there with them—for a moment. For the first time, we feel what they feel—the fear, the terror, the confusion, the doubt, the anger, and the frustration of being caught up in something much bigger than them. We realize that ultimately they are just fighting to survive. For the first time, we experience what it is like to be them, especially when they come home. We begin to "get it." We sense what the soldiers call the "ground truth" of war.

The focus of this book is the mosaic that emerges from a microcosmic look into what it's like to be in the Iraq war. As we look below the surface, even though this new generation of American heroes tells their stories as honestly as they can, we sense the powerful pain of what war does to people. The ultimate question about war begins to surface—"Why is this going on, and when will it end?" There are few legitimate answers. We realize that on a very deep level these American warriors who have done the fighting and seen the dying are still in conflict.

So are we.

It doesn't take a hero to order men into battle. It takes a hero to be one of those men who goes into battle.
—GENERAL NORMAN H. SCHWARZKOPF, retired

DARRYL ANDERSON

Army Specialist
Hometown: Lexington, Kentucky
Lives: Toronto, Canada
Iraq War Service: January 2004–July 2004

I served in Iraq for seven months. While on leave, I went AWOL and moved to Canada. I didn't want to go back. I was having nightmares. I dreamed I saw firefights, my buddies die, kids die. I dreamed I saw myself pulling the weapon on a kid who could have been no more than 12, which I actually did. There was no way he was shooting at us.

I was in Iraq doing this big sacrifice, and I come home and no one even cares. No one understands what we go through. They say, "Oh, thank you for what you've done," but what have I done? . . . Just terrible stuff. If you really cared and really supported me, you'd say, "I'm going to make it so that you don't ever have to go back." That would really be supporting me. Sending me out there for another year and a half is not supporting me. People put those yellow ribbons up and say they support us. I can't see them from Iraq.

A lot of soldiers don't believe in the war or that we should be there, but they are there fighting to stay alive. They thought they were going to be heroes for their country, but now it's just a fight to stay alive. We are poor 18-year-old kids fighting for rich people. Whether we lose or win, I'm still gonna be poor. I'm still not going to have health care.

Even if I go back in and I'm still sane, a lot of the guys who were with me went nuts. I just kept thinking, "You know, I'm not going to be able to stop myself all the time. I am going to kill innocent people, and am I willing to die for this?" They say if we didn't fight, Iraqi terrorists would come in and take over our country. Well, that's exactly what I was doing—busting into people's homes terrorizing families, taking their men. I was a terrorist. If this was the States and Japan hated us, invaded, got rid of Bush, and soldiers came in your house and stomped on you, I would join the resistance even though I don't like Bush. Then I would be the terrorist. We invaded their country. We blew up their homes, and we killed innocent people. What are they going do?

For a long time, it was OK to kill Indians or have slaves, but people stood up and stopped it, and that's what we need to do now. I wasn't willing to fight for something I didn't believe in even if I signed a contract. I can't kill people. I can't go back. In the end, I was disgusted and embarrassed by what I did. I knew I couldn't go back, so my choices were prison or hiding out. My mother called a Toronto lawyer, and they found a place for me. I'm glad I came to Canada. It was not a hard decision to make. My unit went back to Iraq. I haven't been in touch with anyone.

* * *

I joined the army because I didn't have the means to get into college or anything, so I just worked dead-end jobs. To get an education in my world, your best bet was to join the army. I thought, you know, if I joined the army, I'd be helping people. I wouldn't be the bad guy, but one of the good guys. I was 20 and lived with my mother and stepfather in Lexington, Kentucky. I also have a daughter, and I figured if I went into the army, I could really take care of her. I thought if I did that I could be something great, you know. I could be a hero. I thought, "What else could I do? Hang out on the block like every other young American doing nothing?" I felt by joining, I could be somebody.

I joined the army to be a medic. I went to medic school, but I failed the test, and they reclassified me to artillery and combat arms. I liked it better. I did all the training and then was sent to Germany, and then we were sent to Iraq in January of 2004.

I was excited to go. I wanted to see what war was. I wanted to see combat. I was pumped to fight a war, but as soon as I got there to fight, it was like, "What I'm I doing?" When we got there, it was terrible. We lived in bombed-out buildings. We were just basically occupying them. We served as police in different sections. We drove through the area, swept for IEDs [improvised explosive device], did car stops. It was obvious when we got there that there were no weapons of mass destruction, and the people really didn't want us there. People screamed at us, "Go home, go home." They'd shoot at us every day. Kids and men threw rocks at us. It was a concrete jungle, total urban warfare, guerrilla warfare; and the pockets of insurgency were so precise in their methods.

The Iraqi people didn't like what we were doing. We sped down one-way streets on the wrong side. We stormed into anyone's house we wanted. We captured and sent off to prison anyone we wanted.

But it was very hard on us guys. We'd go days without sleeping. We would shower every couple of days, wash our clothes every few weeks. Just do enough to keep alive. I was usually up all night. I'd sleep on a cot. There were five guys to one room. No air conditioning and 130 degrees. Every morning I got up and drove around looking for land mines, but the only way we found them was when they blew up. So every morning we were just waiting to die. Every night we could get hit by mortar attacks. It was death every day. We got so caught up in it. When an attack came, the RPGs [rocket-propelled grenades] they used were so slow and low we saw them and moved out of the way We cheered when they missed us.

There was no day off. Every day, we had our weapons in our hands. I didn't even want to talk to people back home when I was there. What could they say? "Oh, what did you do last night?" and my answer would be, "Oh, I was up on top of a building waiting to shoot people." I felt like I wasn't myself. I was someone else. I would do anything to survive. It was just weird.

* * *

In war, people do horrible things. This one Iraqi guy had a really small foot, and he was struggling to stay on his feet, leaning against the wall, trying to get away from us. My fellow soldiers were yelling at him to keep moving. Everyone is like, "I hate Iraqis." I would even say it. I was racist against them. We all were. That's not how I was raised, to hate people because of their skin color or make fun of them, but that's what we all were doing. We made it OK in our minds. We were all so racist, even the black guys did it. Some of the guys even talked about beating the Iraqis to death.

The first time we got attacked, and a couple of soldiers died, we were like every car that comes down the road and doesn't stop, we are going to fire at. But this is downtown Baghdad, and cars were coming down the street with families in them. This one car came down to where my checkpoint was, and it didn't stop. There were sparks coming from the car. I saw there was a family inside—a mother and two small kids who were like four or five. They had a hard time slowing down, and my supervisor asked, "Why didn't you open fire?" I told him that I could see it was a family, and he told me that the next time I don't open fire, I was going to get in trouble. But I wasn't going to do it. I'd rather a car bomber kill me than I kill an innocent family. I wouldn't shoot unless I could see where it was coming from. I know a guy who shot up a whole family in a traffic stop. He was upset, but all you could say to him was you're sorry. He was going to have to live with it for the rest of his life.

4

* * *

I was part of a combat-ready team. We had to be ready in five minutes to go out. One time we got the alert, and I ran out with two big machine guns in my hands. When I got to the humvee, another guy beat me to the gunner position, and so I handed him the machine guns and got into the vehicle. We were in a humvee with no armor. We came under attack, and the gunner was hit and fell on us. We took his gear off, and someone had to go up there. No one wants to go up, but I decided I would. So I climbed up, pointed my weapon, fired, and nothing happens. I had it on safety, so I take the safety off and aimed in the exact same direction. This time I saw the gun was pointed at some kid who was running. I didn't shoot. I was in a panic because we were under attack and I almost shot this kid. Luckily the gun was on its safety the first time. Next thing a bomb blew up in our faces. There was not enough room for me to duck, and all this stuff hits me. I felt this burning in my side, and I pulled out a bloody, burning piece of metal from my body. Suddenly my legs got weak, and I just fell in the vehicle.

They gave me a Purple Heart for that, which was cool. If it just went a bit further, I could have been sent home. If it moved a bit to one side, I could have been on a [colostomy] bag for the rest of my life.

I was OK, so they taped me up, and we raided a mosque that night. We didn't catch nobody; we never did. It was so unorganized. People think the American army is some great elite force, but what we do is kick down the door and scare everybody, show them a picture, say a name, and they're like, "Oh, he lives down the street." So then we leave and go down the street and look for the guy. Our intel [intelligence] was bad.

I was sent back to my base in Germany in July and went home to visit my mother for Christmas. We were going to be sent back to Iraq in about seven months. I was pretty messed up, and so she got me to Canada where there is a whole support system in place to help us guys who don't want to go back. It seems like all the time you hear of more guys coming to Canada. The people here really support us and want to help us.

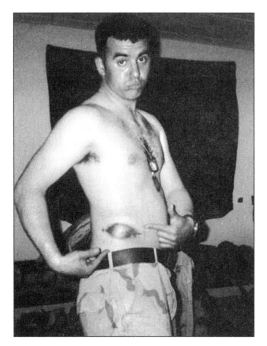

It's hard for guys to get out of the military even when their time is up. I had this one friend who really didn't want to go back, and he was due to come out of the army. But when we got home the army was being really nice to him. They wanted him to reenlist. When you get back from Iraq, you have a lot of money in your bank account. Some people had like $25,000, and they offered you more money to reenlist. When you see that money, you stop thinking about Iraq. My friend said he needed to finish off paying for his motorcycle, so he reenlisted, and now he's unhappy again and probably back in Iraq.

I'm pretty happy because I'm actually doing something positive now. I've talked to thousands of people about my experiences, and people have hugged me and thanked me for what I'm doing. I went to Iraq to help the people there, and I wasn't helping, but now I'm actually helping to stop the war and make the Iraqi people's lives better. Iraq War veterans who speak out against the war are called cowards. I believe in America; I believe in my country. If you speak out against the war, you're considered to be unpatriotic, but I have to speak out against the war. I still dream about it. I can't stop thinking about it.

SAMUEL WHITE

Marine Reserves Sergeant

Lives: Annapolis, Maryland

Iraq War Service: August 2004–April 2005

This is my country. I wake up every day, and I think I am so glad I am an American. Yeah, we have problems. A lot of countries don't like us, but for the most part, we are a good country with good people, who do a lot of good in this world. I can't put into words how much I love this country.

I served in the marines for four years and got out August 28, 2001. In 2003, I got called back, to go to Iraq. I had gotten out less than two weeks before September 11. But the day before we were supposed to leave for Iraq, they told us we were not going. I was like, "You got to be kidding me." I called several other units and said, "I'm ready to go. Take me." It ended up not happening. We just sat around for three months, and then I got out in June of 2003. I felt a void. I felt like a baseball player ready to bat, but the hitter before him strikes out and the game is over.

One night, I was over at a friend's house watching the movie *Black Hawk Down*,[1] and I'm thinking while I'm watching, "I gotta get over there, I gotta get over there." That night I prayed to God that I could go to Iraq. Whatever the different ideologies on the war, I wasn't concerned with it. I am so in love with this country. I was like, "Man, I have to do my part." I knew I could do some good over there. I wanted to be part of it. I wanted to fight for my country. It's not that I take enjoyment out of killing people, but you sign up for a reason: to go to war. I had all this training, but it never was put to the test. Would I live in combat? Am I good enough or lucky enough? I went to bed that night and I prayed.

The next morning my cell phone rang. A Kansas City unit called to see if I'd join their unit and serve in Iraq to replace casualties. I said, "Yes, I'd do it." They gave me a squad of young marines who didn't know anything, and they were mine to mold and teach. I went over to Iraq, and it was an amazing experience, every minute of it, the good and the bad.

I was a scout in back of a vehicle that was a smaller version of a tank. The vehicle would take us as far as it could, and then we would deploy on foot and do combat patrols.

First place we went to, I didn't like it. There wasn't anything going on. We were just sitting in lawn chairs reading books in the middle of nowhere. The nearby town was supposed to be a haven for insurgents, but we saw nothing there. I would have felt fine walking the street there by myself at 2 A.M. Then we got a call to go to Fallujah.[2] I felt this was going to be it. It was weird. We were all scared, but we were all happy. We knew we were going into combat, but we knew this was what we were supposed to do. Our unit was the first unit into Fallujah. Our job was to fight our way through the peninsula all the way to the river. There were hundreds of insurgents in the area. We set up a blockade, and we would go house to house.

---

[1] A movie based on the U.S. raid on Mogadishu, Somalia, in 1993.
[2] Iraqi town where fierce fighting between American soldiers and insurgents took place.

It was intense; it was crazy. Some of things we did . . . war is not a pretty thing. I had my marines I needed to take care of. I got out of it with not one of my marines wounded or killed. I'd like to think of it as skill, but 99 percent of it was luck.

We didn't know who was an insurgent and who wasn't. Someone could drive up to us in their car and wave, and we'd be like, "Oh, that's nice" and wave back, and then they drive the car close to us and blow it up. They'd shoot at you and run away. They didn't want to man up. I'd run in the streets and try to provoke them. Their tactics weren't good. It was frustrating because it was like, "Here I am—come get me."

I was awed the first time I saw a car bomber. I was saying to myself, "What good could they possibly be doing? They would come up to us, and we were in LRVs,[3] small version of tanks. If I were going to lay down my life, I'd want to make sure, at the very least, I would be doing some harm, but we wouldn't let them get close enough to hurt us. I remember one guy blew himself up, and I went over to the car and looked at his dead body and was like, "What did you give your live up for?" When I saw that dead Iraqi, first thing I thought was what a waste of a life. If they love their country so much, why are they killing their own people? They honestly believe they are doing the right thing. I was bewildered at how they think. How is driving their car into a group of women, men, and children doing the right thing and going to win the favor of the people?

I saw a lot of dead bodies. You'd drive in the road, and there would be dead bodies lying there. Some we killed; some we have no idea—they were just lying there. Others killed themselves, in a car bomb.

One time we went into this town that had insurgents, and we were there to hand out candy. I was walking along and stepped on something. I looked down and something was sticking out under my foot. I brushed it off and saw that I was standing on a rigged IED [improvised explosive device]. My life flashed in front of my

---

[3]Light reconnaissance vehicles.

eyes. I was just waiting for the thing to go off. Then I thought if the insurgents were here, I would already be dead. It was a daisy chain IED, which means the insurgents connected all these land mines. When one goes off, it sets the rest of them off, but it didn't go off. Well, it was rigged around a soccer field, and these kids played there. I went over to the guy who was standing by the field and said, "Did you know that this was out there?" He said, "Yes." And I said, "Why didn't you tell us?" He said he was scared. I told him, "If one of my marines would have gotten hurt, you would have been personally responsible, and furthermore, you are protecting people who set up a daisy chain mine field around the place where we see kids play every single day."

An IED is not sophisticated, but they get pretty cunning about it. Don't know when or how they are going to go off. My friend lost both his legs over there. He's in a long-term outpatient facility. My friend, he is not for the war. I asked him if he was mad, and he said, "Sam, I'm the one who volunteered. Back in 1998, I'm the one who signed my name on the bottom line. I'm the one who was living with my wife in southern California and said, 'I'll go back in,' and it happened that I got hurt. The marines are taking care of me. It sucks that I lost my legs, but I put myself in this situation."

I really respected him a lot more. People desert or protest the war; you know, you are definitely entitled to your opinion, but you put your name on the line and said, "You send me anywhere you want to send me."

The first time I killed someone, we had just gotten into Fallujah, and we got engaged from across the river. I saw this person firing at me, and I thought, "This is it, this it." I put my eye on the scope, looked at him, and saw his face. I had a red tracer round, which means you can see the bullets go. I sat there for a second, fired, and I missed him. I waited a second more, and I fired again. I saw the tracer go up in an arc and down through his chest, and that was it. One guy said, "Sgt. White, Sgt. White, you got one of them." It was a weird feeling. I had taken someone's life, but I can't say that I had a whole lot of remorse. I felt adrenaline. I felt power, because I got him before he got me. My marines saw me do that, and so it gave me more credibility. But I don't have nightmares about it. I know for a fact that I killed five. Then, we probably as a unit did another 10 to 20 people, where we all fired together.

One guy I killed was a swimmer. They told us the insurgents were coming at us, and they were swimming to get to us. I was sitting on the roof, with my rifle, and I looked down at them. What we were trying to do was fire at them in way to keep them on the other side, but this guy kept coming across. I said it was like shooting fish in a barrel, but I almost wanted him to go back the other way. I felt it was a cheesy way to kill somebody while they are swimming—you know, sitting on those chairs on the roof and shooting the people like target practice. It was surreal; sometimes I couldn't believe what I was doing. But we were given our orders. They knew we were coming. We even told them if they were male, they had no business to be in Fallujah unless they were insurgents. If I had nothing to do with the insurgency, I would get out of town even if I was poor. I could be poor somewhere else.

One of my friends got killed outside of Ramadah. His unit was coming to our position on the main highway, and an IED went off. It was a well-placed IED, and it went through the vehicle armor and pierced my friend's head. His eye came out. I remember I didn't even know it happened. When we came back to our base, they told me he was dead. It was like I was sitting there, and I was like trying not to cry. I'm a marine. They can't see me cry. I put my sunglasses on, tried to keep my eyes open. I was just talking to him on the radio, and then, damn, he's dead. He had a young wife, a young kid, and a newborn. That really sucked. We had his memorial, and they had his weapon, helmet with his picture on it on display. They played "Amazing Grace," and everyone was crying, but I couldn't let myself cry because I was Sgt. White. I knew all the answers. I was the one that kept them going. I have never cried about it. Two kids will grow up without their dad, and a young wife will not have her husband. As bad as my life can get, at least I'm still alive.

I was there for eight months. I remember when we were leaving, we were getting in the plane, and a bunch of guys were getting off. I made eye contact with one, and he had this look on his face

like, "Oh, my God. I'm in Iraq," and I just nodded at him and said, "It will be OK, buddy."

When we touched down, it was the culmination of everything. I remember touching my foot down on the ground and thinking, "I made it back. I made it back." Fire truck sirens were going crazy, and they were shooting off water. They were playing the "Marine Hymn." I started tearing up. We made it. All my marines made it. Everyone was so happy.

I support President Bush going in and everything he did. I'd rather be fighting over there than over here. I think it's something we needed to do. We need to stay the course. We could get the job done with the same amount of troops, but it would be faster with more, and easier. We are combating the insurgents while trying to facilitate a new government. They are having the same problems we had while putting together the Declaration of Independence. It's going to take time. More people will die, more innocent people will die, and anyone who thinks otherwise is crazy. Anyone who thinks in five years we are just going to leave is crazy. We have had a military presence in every country we have had a conflict with. In the end, it will come out good. I know we are doing a good thing and made a difference. We have to stay, if for no other reason than we are already in too far, and we can't pull out now. If we do, it would be in vain for every person who laid his or her life down.

I saw progress when I was there. People were helping us out more. Tribes started their own guard to look for insurgents. More Iraqis were showing up for training. I saw things we were rebuilding and repairing. I don't mind people having an opinion. I just hate when they don't know what they are talking about.

The people here in Annapolis, where I was a bartender and junior at the University of Maryland, the whole time were sending me stuff. They had donation nights at different bars, and they sent us $5,000 worth of stuff. When I came back, I had a party at McGarvey's, where I work as a bartender. They put signs with pictures of me on every telephone pole, inviting people to the party. It said "Sam's Back. Come to His Party." And then these kids from a very liberal school ripped all of them off. It's cool if they didn't believe in the war, but it takes their credibility away. To me, that's not protesting. That's hate, and I am out there risking my life. They should have respect for that. Maybe not for what I'm doing or why we are over there, but respect for the fact that I am a person, just like they are.

LADDA TAMMY DUCKWORTH

National Guard Major

Lives: Hoffman Estates, Illinois

Iraq War Service: February 2004–November 2004

I am not going to dishonor the effort in saving my life by saying, "Woe is me, I got no legs." Well, I got one knee. There are guys who have none, guys who are blind. I have my arms, my face, my brain. This is a pretty good life I have compared to what it could be. Plus they make prosthetic high heels. I checked into it. Not three-inch stilettos, but at least an inch or two of heel. I'll be good to go.

I am so grateful to be alive. I should be dead. A person with a femur artery cut should bleed out in 4½ minutes, and I survived for 20. My crewmembers thought I was dead. They carried me, dragged me. They fell down. I was a bloody mess, and they got me help in 15 minutes after the insurgents attacked us. When I got to the medevac helicopter, I wasn't given first aid. They thought I was dead. I was laying on my crew chief, and he was the first person to suspect I might be alive. He felt my blood bleeding on him, and it was warm. He thought maybe my heart was still pumping. He said, "Check her—I think she is still alive." The human body can hold, depending on your size, six to seven units of blood. They gave me 40 units of blood in the first 24 hours. I should not be here. I'm not depressed or upset. The alternative to this is death.

* * *

I was in command of a National Guard air assault helicopter company in Chicago. After 9/11, it became more real than ever that I needed to train my men for war. As a company commander, it weighs even more heavily on you that you have a responsibility. In December 2003, we were activated. I was not originally slated to go to Iraq. I was put in a different battalion to help bring them up to standards for a future deployment. But I called my commander up and said, "Listen, please take me. I can't be one of the only aviation officers in this state standing here waving good-bye to the unit as it goes to war. Please take me." It ended up they needed me anyway, so I got to go.

My position was battle captain assistant operation officers. I ran the tactical operations center day to day. I did everything that needed to be done each day. That freed my boss, the operations officer, to do planning. He could work on next week's major mission, and I would take care of things day to day. I had a computer network and would coordinate all the missions. I'd assist them and do briefings. My job was when they went out to fly, I'd make sure things went as smoothly as possible. I worked in a trailer with a network of computers.

I begged to fly. It's important if you are going to send people out there to fly a mission, you need to be willing to go out there and fly a mission. I flew missions twice a week.

Ninety-five percent of what we did was movement of troops and supplies. It was the safest way to get around Iraq. We were moving bodies and blood, whatever needed to move from one place to another. I went as far north as the border with Jordan and Syria, up to the border to Iran, south, to Abu Ghraib. That's how people got around. You never knew what your mission would be any day.

I was there for more than eight months before the shootdown.

I had been shot at with antiaircraft missiles on one of my missions, and it missed us. We had instances where our crews had been shot at and that kind of thing, but we had not had any hostile fire or any major instances where people were injured. Mine was the first.

I had spent the day flying missions in support of the First Cavalry Division in Baghdad. I was constantly going over the Baghdad area moving people, food, supplies, anything you could think of. We were there all day long. I probably reported to duty at 4 A.M., took off at 7 A.M., and then spent the whole day until about 4 P.M. flying. We had completed our mission and were headed back to base. We flew over basically a nest of insurgents. This is around the time of the battle of Fallujah, and basically a nest of insurgents had gotten out of Fallujah, and they were north of Baghdad. We happened to fly over them. Some other aircraft had flown over the exact same spot five minutes before us and got fired on, but we didn't know that. It hadn't been reported. So the bad guys were waiting for another aircraft to fly over them, and here we came. They shot everything they had into the air, small arms fire, AK-47s, RPGs [rocket-propelled grenades]—everything—and at least one of the RPGs hit us, and it hit me. It exploded right between my legs. It came up right through the Plexiglas window beneath my feet and exploded between my legs, and the shrapnel went through the roof of the aircraft and out the door. We flew without doors on because it was hot. It was a blessing because if the doors had been on, it would have kept the blast in on me, and I probably would have been killed. But with the doors off, some of the blast dissipated out the aircraft. It amputated both my legs immediately. It took off most of my right arm, but I didn't know that. I wasn't flying—the other pilot was. I had just given him the command. I had been flying all day. So he had taken the controls and was physically flying the aircraft, and I was coordinating with air traffic. I heard the tap, tap, tap on my side on the fuselage, and I said, like, "Hey, I think we've been hit." As soon as I said that, there was a giant fireball in front of my face. He never responded to my initial comment, and the crew chief on my side and the gunner on my left side didn't respond to me, either. What had happened was the RPG took out our radio communications. We couldn't talk to each other, and we couldn't talk to anybody outside the aircraft. It also it took out all of our instruments. So the electronics running my instruments were completely blank. I had no cockpit indications to tell me what was going on in the aircraft. Because of that, no one responded, and I thought I was the only one who was alive or uninjured. I thought I was the only person capable of flying the aircraft at the time, and I tried to land it. I got on the controls. I don't remember passing out. I could have been passing in and out. We were flying right above the treetops, and there was a big danger of the aircraft hitting the trees and crashing, so my concentration went immediately to flying the aircraft. All my training took over, and it was almost like my body responded to the incident before my brain or the rest of me comprehended the situation.

I picked a landing spot. The cockpit was filled with smoke; the aircraft was shaking like crazy. I had no indications on the condition of the aircraft. I was listening to the engine on my side. The sound changed, so I knew it had probably sucked up some of the shrapnel and metal. So I thought I was going to lose an engine. I was fighting the emergency at that point, trying to land the aircraft. As soon as the aircraft landed on the ground, I saw grass coming up through the aircraft, and I knew that we landed. I was confused. The aircraft sits a good five feet above ground, so to see grass coming up means we would have landed so hard that we would have crushed the ground. I was indignant that there was grass coming through, and I couldn't figure out why that was. I remember thinking I had to shut down the engine and do an emergency engine shutdown review to fight any detectable fires. I remember thinking I had to reach up to do that, and then, just raising my hand, I passed out.

What really happened was, I was the most severely injured. The pilot of the aircraft was on the controls, thank God, and stayed on them. If I had been on the controls, if I had been flying up to five minutes prior to this, we would have crashed. I don't know why these things happened to save my life, but they did. He was on the controls and landed the aircraft. We both picked the same landing spot. When I told him what I went through, he was thinking all the same things. He was not injured. His eyebrow was burnt off from the explosion that happened on me. The crew chief behind me almost lost his leg, but there was a sliver of bone left, and the doctors here pinned it all together, and then the bone grew back. The crew chief on my left side, a young kid and great guy, had a bullet come through his tailbone, and so he has a bullet stuck in his butt. They left it in. He is 22 and a college student, so now he is a combat-wounded war hero with a Purple Heart and a scar to show the girls in the bars. He is doing fine, and I have been here at Walter Reed ever since. They got me here on November 14.

I was so badly injured that my status was reported to my husband as a possible triple amputee. The doctors in both Baghdad and Germany thought I would lose the arm, but they got me here within 50 hours of being hit, and they knew if anyone could save my arm, the doctors here could—and they did. So, fortunately, I am only a double amputee, not a triple.

I was unconscious for 11 days, and for those 11 days, it was like I was asleep, but I could still hear a voice telling me, "You are injured. You are OK. You are at Walter Reed. You are home." That was my husband's voice. For 11 days, he kept saying that to me even though I was unconscious. So I knew I was OK. It was like a mantra going on in my head.

When I woke up, my legs hurt. I was in so much pain. I said, "Please, can I have some painkillers for my feet and my legs?" That's when he had to tell me that I lost my legs. I was devastated as soon my husband told me I lost my legs. I didn't know why exactly I was there, but as soon as he said that, it was like a trigger, and all the memories came back of struggling to land the aircraft. I thought that I had crashed the aircraft. I thought that I lost my legs because I did not complete the landing, that I was too focused on the stupid grass and had rolled the aircraft on the side and lost my legs. I thought I deserved to lose my legs if I didn't do my job as a pilot and crashed the aircraft. I was devastated that I had injured my crew chief behind me. These people depended on me to land the aircraft, and I didn't do a good job. I kept it to myself for a few days, and I finally broke down. I was crying, and my husband asked me what was wrong, and I told him. He told me that I was hit by an RPG, and it amputated my legs immediately. I didn't know that my legs were gone when I tried to land it. I remember being frustrated that the aircraft was not responding to my pedal inputs. When he told me that, it was a huge weight that was lifted off of me. Then, I was going into surgery, and my crew chief was in the gurney next to me waiting to go in. I was so happy to see him.

✶ ✶ ✶

The pain was very bad in the beginning, so bad that all I could do was count, "One one thousand . . . two one thousand . . . ," for each minute. They gave me morphine, but it did nothing for me except make me hallucinate and vomit. The first four or five days, I couldn't sleep. I hurt so bad. I can't describe it, but another soldier who'd been blown up understands, and there was a soldier who lost her arm, standing there with me, by my bed counting with me. That's what people did for me—they counted with me.

My first words to my husband when he told me I was OK, were "Put me back to work toward my rehabilitation." I have not gone through anger or denial—you know, all the stages of grief. I haven't gone through any of that because I was fighting until the end. They put tissue from my chest, down to my ribs and abdomen, to save my arm, which I have problems with. I don't have a lot of strength. I can't feel my pinky, but I can make a fist now, which I couldn't before. I couldn't put up my hair when I was first going through rehabilitation. I couldn't use this arm at all. The goal was to get me to be able to put up my hair in a ponytail and put on my own earrings. I'm such a girl. I'm such a girly girl. My favorite color is pink. It's so funny.

✫ ✫ ✫

When I was going through ROTC and I was getting ready to be commissioned, we get to request what job you wanted. For all the guys, three of the top five choices had to be combat branches. But women didn't have to do that because women were barred from combat at that time. The only combat job I knew I had a shot at was combat aviation. I wanted a combat job not because I wanted to go into combat, but I didn't think it was fair that three out of their top five choices had to be combat jobs. How could I be an equal soldier if I didn't take equal risk? At the time, it was 1992; there was a lot of debate about allowing women in combat. In 1993, they finally let female aviators into combat.

I was lucky I got it, and I loved it. We say that you strap the aircraft on your back, and I did. I'm controlling this giant assault helicopter, and I'm flying through the air, and there are guys who depend on me, and I depend on them. It's amazing, the most amazing feeling. It's not a soaring-through-the-air kind of thing. It's down and dirty, a heavy beast of a machine that I control. What other country would let me do that? Not that many. I am a minority female who got to be a company commander. You know, for all the stuff that goes on in this country, I was given that opportunity, and I am so lucky to have been able to do that.

✫ ✫ ✫

I was an army brat. My father worked for the UN in Southeast Asia and later for oil companies. He went to Thailand during the Vietnam War and fell in love with the region and with my mother, who is Thai. I was born in Thailand and grew up in Southeast Asia. I moved to Hawaii for the last half of my senior year.

I was getting my master's degree at George Washington University, and I was specializing in strategic studies and international affairs, and I realized all my friends were either current military, prior military, or guardsman, that sort of thing. I was really intrigued by it, and they encouraged me to at least try out for ROTC

and get a better understanding of the military, so I did. I really enjoyed it. My dad served in World War II and Vietnam. He pushed my brother to be in the military, but not me. So when I went home and joined ROTC, his only comment was "Do you think that you'll make it?"

When I graduated, my mother cried. She was like, "I raised you to be a girl. I put you in stockings and lace. What are you doing wearing combat boots?" But both my parents grew to be very proud of me. I was commissioned in 1992. Never been on active duty, always a reservist or a guardsman.

I like the fact that I can serve my country. I know that's a corny thing to say, but I think, growing up overseas, I lived in a lot of war-torn countries. I lived in Cambodia and saw refugees. I saw pictures of Amerasian Vietnamese children who were street urchins, just thrown out into the street because they were Amerasian. I thought, "But for the grace of God, that could be me living on the streets as a beggar."

I lived in countries that had no freedom of speech. I lived in countries that if you wore the national colors on your tube socks, you could get in trouble. I feel extremely grateful to be an American, and I believe that everyone needs to serve our communities and country in some way. I was just privileged enough to do it in the military. It's vital to give back to this great country even though there are a lot of things that are screwed up. We have are own problems, but for what we have, we should give back.

So I got in the military, and I enjoyed the camaraderie, the friends that I made, and the value system. I just wanted to do my 20 years.

* * *

Therapy is going well. People who had been injured like me started visiting my family before I even woke up and then visiting me to show me where they were in their recovery. They were walking with their prosthetic leg and moving their prosthetic arms, and I was like, "I can do this." I am doing well. I come to the hospital do my exercises, put my legs on, and leave my wheelchair behind. It's just a matter of building up endurance every day.

I testified in front of the Senate Committee on Veterans Affairs. They want to close all the military hospitals Stateside so that once you're treated in Germany and come back, you immediately would go to a regular hospital near your home. That way, you'd get to live at home and be close to your family. I told them that if I could get the same amount of care, if the care and support were equal at a civilian or VA hospital close to home, of course I would support it, but I don't think I would. There is nothing like being here [at Walter Reed Army Hospital] in that room, on the third floor, with 40 other recent amputees going through the same thing. If I were sent home, I would be one of maybe two amputees from the war in the entire state, and the doctors and therapists would not have the experience like here. They have seen 340 cases here. Take those 340 cases and split them up among the 50 states—the expertise would not be built up. It's tough being away from home, but I am getting such specialized care here.

* * *

I would like to stay in the Army National Guard and get back in the cockpit. As a senior ranking officer, my days of flying were behind me, anyway. Flying was not my primary job, but I wasn't done yet. And I am not going to let some guy with an RPG, some insurgent, decide how I am going to live my life. If I stop flying, it's because I decided to stop, not because an insurgent decided. I'm going to get back in that cockpit. It's probably going to take two to three years of rehabilitation and training, but I am going to do it. I just completed 14 years in the military. I could retire now, get a medical retirement, but I want to finish. I still have a commitment to the guard, and I don't think I'm done doing my job.

I work for Rotary International, a nonprofit. I managed a department that provided administrative services for Rotaries in the Pacific. I traveled to Asia a lot. They are holding my job for me.

I miss my body. I miss my strong, healthy body. The first time it hit me, I was watching a triathlon, and this man, an arm amputee, was doing it, and it made me cry. I was like, "I want a healthy body." I am addicted to *America's Next Top Model*. I don't know why. I love Tyra Banks. I think she is the greatest. I am addicted to that show. Sometimes I'm like, "I can't wear stilettos anymore." And when I go shopping, I have to compensate for how my legs look under my clothes. But then those feelings go away.

We will have a big party here at Walter Reed on my one-year anniversary—my alive day. It will be great. I am very blessed. I have a good employer, a good husband who has been here for me. I appreciate every day of my life.

IVAN MEDINA

Army Chaplain's Assistant

Lives: Verona, New York

Iraq War Service: September 2002–August 2003

I lost the one person I loved so much and meant so much to me in the world, my twin brother Irving. The vehicle he was driving hit an IED [improvised explosive device]. They said he died quickly. They said he didn't suffer, but I know he did—he just didn't show it. The last time I talked to my brother, we made plans for when he was coming back and how he was going to get out of the military. Then he was taken away from me . . . in one day, everything was taken away from me. The condolence letters that [Secretary of Defense Donald] Rumsfeld and the president sent did not even look signed. They were stamped. It made me so angry, so pissed off. They were saying, "We don't care about you personally."

I speak out in my brother's name. I served in Iraq, and I want people to know the truth. I consider this my country. We grew up here, and we love it here. I believe in America, and all I want is that if we go to war again, that it will be for the right reason, that we ask the right questions and not fight in a war that should never have happened. My mission now is to get our troops home alive. If I can save one American soldier or one Iraqi child, it will be worth it. If I can make a better future, then my brother will live forever.

* * *

My family moved to the United States from Mexico City when I was around six years old.

My sister had joined the military when I was in high school. I needed college money, and for many generations, my family was in the military in their country. For my siblings and me, it was a way to give thanks to our adoptive country. We wanted to wear the uniform, which most Americans didn't do. I joined in March of 2001. My brother Irving and I joined together. We took the test together, and we originally signed up together. They offered us the chaplain assistant position, and they told me, "You'll never see the front lines. You'll be able to go to school and work." So we signed up.

Irving was hesitant at first right from the start. He wasn't sure he wanted to be a chaplain assistant. A few days before we were supposed to go into basic training, he said he didn't want to go. I told him, "Then don't go, but I'm going." The day we were supposed to report, my brother dropped me off near the recruiting station and said, "Good luck, and I love you. Take care of yourself." And I said, "You do the same." He hugged me, and then he left. The recruiter asked me where he was, and I said I didn't know. I didn't want to tell them, but I said he didn't want to go and . . . and then they started calling my house and calling my friends. After that, the recruiter was constantly calling the house and going to his community college until they finally convinced him to go in.

I came home for our 20th birthday. We went to a restaurant, and they bought us a cake. We looked a lot alike for the first time, really, since we both had shaved heads. I was proud of him. A few weeks later, I started my career being a chaplain assistant, which was basically being a social worker for the soldiers, taking care of their religious needs, precounseling them, setting up for church services, and things like that. The first year of my enlistment, I loved it. I really did. My chaplain said, "If we go to war, you are the person I want to come with me." I said, "Sir, if we are going to fight Al Qaeda, I'll be right there with you."

I had pride in those days. I was on the base on September 11. To me, being a twin, the twin towers represented my life. My father used to say, "That's you and your brother there." I had a lot of anger because to me, that attack was against people who could not defend themselves. We as a military are trained to defend and fight. We knew Al Qaeda did it. I would have gone to Afghanistan and fought the Taliban and Al Qaeda network because they were responsible for 9/11, and it would have been a great pride and honor to do it.

We weren't sent to Afghanistan. Some units went, but not all of us. I was working for a garrison unit—we run the base when everyone is gone. In August 2002, they transferred me from the garrison unit to an engineering unit in Fort Stewart that was part of the Third Infantry Division.

They told me the day that I was transferring that, by the way, you are going to be deployed to Kuwait for six months. I went to my new chaplain captain and said I needed to go on leave. I wanted to see my family and say good-bye to them. I went back home for two weeks around Labor Day weekend.

I told them I was going to be deployed for six months or until mission completed. The drums of war were beating. My sister and brother also came up. It was the last time as a family we were all together. I was happy we were all together. My sister left before my brother did. My brother and I got into an argument, and we didn't speak, and my brother didn't even want to say good-bye.

I remember my father told him to go into my bedroom to say good-bye to me, which he then did. I didn't know it was the last time I would see him in my whole life. I didn't know he would be killed in Iraq. To this day I regret how we said good-bye that day.

My unit left three days after Labor Day in 2002. I was thinking to myself, "Wow, I can say I've been in the Middle East, but it'll be hot and I'll be in the middle of nowhere, and I won't get to see my family in a long time." I was in a new unit, and I was trying to befriend my comrades and see what their needs were. I felt like an outsider. We hit the ground in Kuwait and were constantly training, getting ready for war. You would hear that the way home leads through Baghdad, and that we would be there until the mission is accomplished. Around November my chaplain and I went into a meeting. Our colonel said the war plans were done; now all we really had to do was wait for the word.

I would call my parents twice a week, and my father and I would talk about Iraq and what was going on in the world, and he said, "I don't think you are going in. I think he [President Bush] will back down. You'll be fine." Things were classified, but I gave him hints that we were going to go. Then, by December, the entire unit started coming in, the National Guard, the whole entire division, reservists, and reporters.

My father was still saying this is all just show. But by the middle of February, we were sent to the desert near the Iraq border to just be out there. We were taking these jugs of water and taking showers like that. More journalists were being embedded in our unit. Then came the day in March, three or four days before the invasion, when our first sergeant told us that the president was going to address the nation, and then we were going to war.

I remember my soldiers and friends saying we were supposed to be going home instead of to war. We were tired. We wanted to get started so that we could go home. People were anxious.

At 3:30 A.M., we went to brigade headquarters where they had loudspeakers and heard the president's speech. And at 6 A.M., we were moving closer to the border so that we would just be a few minutes away.

I didn't understand why we were going in, and I felt it was for the oil or his father, but not for WMD [weapons of mass destruction] because we didn't know if they had them. I was just hoping that they had them. I wasn't too thrilled, but as a soldier, you didn't question the orders. You just do it. I said, "If we go to war, we are ready for it, and we will follow the orders of the president of the United States."

Two days before we invaded, I got a reporter to lend me a phone so that I could call my mom. It was late afternoon in New York, and my mom said my brother just went back to his base and said they will probably send him to Iraq. I told her I loved her and thanked her for everything she did for me, and I asked her to tell everyone that I loved them. I told her if she didn't hear from me, it was good news, but if you hear something, it will be in the form of a uniform. I said I loved her and that I could not have asked for better parents, and I didn't want them to worry. I told her I'll be back and everything will be OK. She said she wouldn't worry, and then her voice cracked, and I couldn't stand it.

✫ ✫ ✫

The day before the original invasion, Saddam Hussein ordered his soldiers to throw missiles, and one landed close to us. We heard the sirens, and we had to put our chemical suits on. I was running. I never ran so fast in my life. I'll tell you, throughout the training I never thought it could be so fast. They tell you that you have nine minutes, and I never saw people put the chemical suits on so fast. I was so proud of my soldiers. I remember thinking, "What the hell am I doing? I could be home watching this instead of living it."

My commanders said we were ready. I wanted to laugh. Half of my division had no body armor; half had no armor on their vehicles. My vehicle had no armor, and mine was a soft-skin vehicle. The chaplain and I went out to find tarps of metal to put on vehicles. We were running low on water. We were not given a lot of ammunition. I had only six to eight magazines to last me until we got to Baghdad. And so as the sun set, they told us we will see the air force and artillery bomb Iraq, and the artillery would start dismantling the border to make a pathway for us to go in. At night, you saw fire in the sky and heard the bombs dropping. I was amazed.

The next day the infantry went in with our engineers, and we were given the go-ahead to go into Iraq.

We made a sign that said, "Welcome to Iraq Third Infantry Second Brigade." We made it so the soldiers could see it as they went into Iraq.

You see all the Iraqi children and people waving American flags, blowing kisses, asking for food and cigarettes and water, and we were told we were supposed to give them nothing. I wondered if we are liberating them, why can't we help them out? I always did what I thought was right. I threw some bottles of water and MREs [meals ready-to-eat]. And they were really happy.

That night was the first time I had to deal with a soldier's death. He was not killed by enemy fire but by a stupid mistake. It had been about 50, 60 hours into the war, and we were tired and we hadn't slept. If we slept 8 hours in 60, that was a lot. I remember slowing down, and we heard over the radio, "We need a chaplain, we need a chaplain." I called in and went around the other vehicles to see what was going on. There had been an accident. One girl was so tired that she ran into another car. Her passenger was pinned to his seat, and he was dying. He was suffocating. We started performing last rites. He was a really young soldier. He said, "Tell my family I love them and tell them I'm sorry I'm not coming home." Then he died a few minutes after that. It was devastating to me. He was 19. I felt so horrible, but we continued on. The chaplain told me to get some rest. I slept for an hour. After that we encountered firefights. People were so tired they drove their vehicles into a ditch.

I saw firsthand what our bombs did. There were vehicles that were burned. They were not military vehicles but Toyotas with charred skeletons inside. I saw a lot of our smart bombs weren't hitting the targets. There were people in the streets crying because a bomb hit their house, people crying because their loved ones were missing or dead. The Iraqis came around where we were and started picking up the bodies of the people they knew. Women were screaming, and I felt horrible. We saw people crouching into the fighting positions. We didn't see weapons, but we saw there

30

were also women and children with them. They were using their women and children as shields. We tried to leave, so we wouldn't have to do battle with them and put those innocent lives at risk. We'd move on, and we'd hear bullets flying, and we kept going.

We got to our next objective and set up a checkpoint. No one told the Iraqis that putting your hand up meant stop. To some Iraqis, it meant hello. So they didn't know, and we didn't know, and we opened fire on a lot of vehicles on our checkpoints. I remember coming up on one, and a whole family was dead—the father, mother, and the children—and you feel bad and you can't do anything about it. You feel it's their life or your life. We didn't know who the enemy was.

We killed so many innocent people. They said if it moves, you shoot. It doesn't matter. We were not allowed to feed them or give them water, but a lot of times they were grateful for us to be there. The closer we got to Baghdad, the worse it got. More death came; more soldiers' deaths came. I was helping identify bodies, console the injured, giving last rites to soldiers. No one was welcoming us.

We got to a town right outside of Baghdad and took over a building that belonged to Iraqi forces. A bomb hit the building right near where we were. I heard people screaming and crying. I had ringing in my ear. I could see the debris coming down and red and black smoke. It was like watching a war movie. It went so fast and so slow at the same time. People were running out of the building. I ran to the building with a jug of water and a fire extinguisher. What hit the building was a missile. It was one of the last attacks before Saddam went missing. You could smell burned skin all over, and they were bringing out people totally burned. I was looking for the chaplain, and I remember seeing one of my company sergeants, and he was crying, and I was like, "Are you OK?" He said, "They hit us where it hurts. Those bastards hit us."

Then we heard these guns going off. The ammunition we had in the building was going off. We didn't know if it was from there or if we were being attacked. One sergeant major who I thought was great person was so burned, he almost lost an eye. He didn't

care. He kept asking, "How many dead? How many injured? How is everybody?" He wanted to help. To me, that is heroism.

Three soldiers were dead. One was my friend, and he was a father of three. Our last conversation was about how he couldn't wait until this was over to go see his wife and kids. I broke down there and cried in my vehicle. Some of the guys came around me and said, "Are you OK?"

I felt I came so close to being killed. I was like, "You dumb ass. You should have just stayed in college." A lot of people thought my job was the simplest job in the military, but it took so much out of me emotionally.

They didn't tell me this would happen when I was recruited. I learned real quick in Iraq there is no such thing as the front line. Everywhere is the front line in war, whether you are support or infantry. The enemy doesn't distinguish.

We then took over the airport and the ministry of oil. The rest of Baghdad they allowed to be looted. I remember seeing a body bag that was dripping blood. I remember seeing an Iraqi on a gurney screaming about paradise and Allah. I just wanted to grab my gun and shoot him.

They told us at least six times we were going home, then Fallujah happened, and they needed our brigade to deal with it. We stayed there until August. We had one bottle of water to last us through the day. Our vehicle was breaking down making us targets, and we asked for materials to fix them, and they said they can't get them into the country. Every night in Fallujah was a fight, day and night. Bush declared all operations over. Then he said, "Bring it on," and the violence escalated. It made me so mad. Every day, at least one soldier would die after his comments.

I spent my 21st birthday there and tried to find my brother, but I couldn't find him. They sent us home in August of 2003. I spent 11 months in the Middle East.

I came home, and life went back to normal. But then one day, I was coming out of the post office, and I got a phone call from my sister, and I just knew my brother was dead. The whole day I had been feeling bad. Around the time my brother died, I lost my breath. I could not breathe. I felt dizzy all day, and I felt really down. I said, "It's Irving, isn't it? He's dead, isn't he?" and she started crying, and I said, "Tell me it's not true?" and I started crying in my car.

My brother shouldn't have been there. We both shouldn't have been there. I couldn't keep quiet anymore. I felt we went in there for the wrong reasons. I loved my brother so much. I speak out for him, in his name, in his memory.

JOHN BALL JR.

Marine Corporal
Hometown: Pottstown, Pennsylvania
Iraq War Service: February 2003–June 2003

I'm gay, and I served in the marines for four years. I excelled at my job, but I couldn't reenlist because I was scared that if the commanders found out, I would lose everything. So I can't go back until the ban on gays in the military is lifted. So when I see an American flag, I think I don't have the freedoms everyone else has even though I fought for them. I have served my country in war and peace. Then I get out of my selfish mode and think, "Well, there are people who have died for their country, and people that have it far worse than me. At least I got to serve for four years." I think I'm perfect for the military, and it definitely worked for me. I loved it, but when I was there, I always had that feeling that I was going to lose my job because I'm gay. It made me feel like I did something wrong. I could be fired because I'm something I can't control or take away. I know from my life experience that I tried to make it go away, and I would never wish being gay on anyone. If it were a choice, I would not choose it. I'm very angry a lot of the days when I see an American flag, but I have a lot of respect and admiration and pride in people who serve in the military and past vets. Yet, I'm selfish because the government has hurt my life. I know that I shouldn't have to be working at TGI Friday's as a waiter, but I have to deal with it.

*　　*　　*

I was in high school, and I was clearly not college bound and knew I was going to go in the military. I knew I was gay then, but at that point in my life, I didn't fully understand what it meant to be gay. I thought I could turn it off or just deal with it like I have my whole life.

So I thought if I was going to join the military, I should join the one that was going to be the most challenging for me. So I chose the Marine Corps. I enlisted September 26, 2001, right after high school.

I don't even think I looked at someone in basic training. It was three months of retraining your brain how to think—retraining your priorities so you think in a way that works for the military. The hardest part was just getting through. Afterward, I was stationed in Camp Lejeune in North Carolina for four years and deployed twice with an expeditionary unit.

Yeah, being gay was not a big deal. A few times back at the barracks, if someone was drunk, you might hear a comment here and there, but they came from the people you never talked to. You may have worked with them, but that was it. I would walk to my car and hear the *F* word, but it wasn't all the time and not as much as I thought.

Our first lift was a Mediterranean lift, which was a six-months float.[1] No one knew I was gay on the lift. On the second tour we

---

[1]A military convoy of ships.

went with the same group of people. We became a family. We were together for three years. I had been in for four months, so it was big chunk of my enlistment, and they slowly started to know about me. I came out to my best friend in the marines, and he was very OK about it, and he said basically he already knew, and it didn't affect our friendship. He told me he'd watch my back, and I never had a problem. I did my job, and I did what was required of me, and I excelled at my job. I was in communications. I was a radio operator. I went from being a radio operator to a semi-intelligence person, which I didn't have the training for. But the people I worked with were in intelligence, and I was their communicator. I got attached to these people who had no idea how to work any communications equipment, so I basically was the person who took all the intelligence they collected and sent it back to the ship or any place they needed to go.

We were on our way home from a second six-months float when they said we were going to war with Iraq. We didn't think we were going to be part of it. People were upset, but our command wanted to be a part of it. We had the ammunition, the team, and the firepower. We could go out there and kick some butt. I was 50/50. There was a large part of me that said we were ready, and then there was a part of me that knew that for the first ones there, it's always mass confusion and unnecessary death. People are firing back and forth, and the next thing you know, people are dead. I didn't want to die. I was selfish. I wanted to live my life. But they decided to turn us around and send us to a base in Kuwait. We were there one night and started pushing north in a convoy.

It was mass confusion on both sides. Both seemed confused. I'd be driving in a humvee with my rifle and pointing it at kids. I wondered what the kids were going to think later on in life to have a rifle pointed at them when they were six years old. Did they understand? We would go through the towns searching for weapons, and these men would smuggle their stuff with these kids or use them as shields. The kids didn't understand, but they were being used. I felt sorry for them. They would put guns on kids or travel with kids in their arms. They used the kids as shields, but the kids were fearless. The kids would jump on our vehicles, looking for food.

They were starving. We would throw food at them, a cracker, an MRE [meal ready-to-eat]. But once the kids knew we had the food, they would jump on our vehicles, and we would just push them off. And then you'd see the kid just fall on the side of the road, and it would break your heart.

Everything happened so fast. We would be in one town one day and the next day somewhere else. I don't think much got accomplished, and we didn't seem to know what was going on. There was supposed to be all this research about the weapons, but we couldn't find any.

Honestly, I wasn't as scared as I thought I would be. The team I was with was so good at their jobs. They were so professional about everything, trained so well. I trusted everybody.

I saw a lot of things in Iraq. I saw people tied up on the side of the road or just dead. It was a shock to see people like that. We came in there and, in some cases, ruined their lives. Some people there had a life. They had jobs, food, and their kids. But when we came, they were starving. They had no jobs. There was no order. Their lives changed, and they were very angry. They said it was our fault. They didn't have televisions. They didn't know what was happening, but they knew before we came, they had a life. But now they didn't. I saw women screaming and crying with their babies. I couldn't understand what they were saying, but I knew what they were saying: "What are you doing here? My babies are hungry. Why? Why? Why? When is this going to stop?"

We had no plan to feed them. We were letting them starve to death. You just can't go in a place and disrupt their lifestyle and not have a way to restore order quickly.

These people had no food, and the government had no plan. We should have never done it without a plan. It really bothered me. These innocent people—they are not killers, and we can't take care of them. War is not perfect. I know that, but whoever made the plans for this war did a horrible job. Being on the ground level, I didn't see any weapons of mass destruction, so I wasn't sure of what we were doing.

We went from town to town, but there was nothing. The way we were treated in each town was so different. In one town they threw rocks and all kinds of things at us. They were sending kids at us to steal our rifles and vehicles. We pushed them away. Some people were very angry. Then we went to another town, and the people screamed we were heroes and dropped to their knees thanking us. They said stuff like, "You are saving us from this guy we have been under for so long. Thank God there is hope for our country." Those were the people who were intelligent and saw that five years from now it will be a different place. We went into towns and saw the American flag waving, and it always gave me goose bumps. There were pictures of Saddam on the ground, his eyes scratched out. They really hated him. We were constantly reminded of him. But those who were starving wanted to kill us. There was no instant gratification. You'd move forward, then feel you were moving backward. Toward the end of my time there, they were finally bringing in supplies for the people.

People didn't talk about me being gay. We were just helping each other. Most of the sad parts were when people missed their kid's birthday or were missing a spouse. They would break down—not for long, but it pushed them to their breaking point. There were about four females in my unit, and they did their job when they were supposed to. The guys weren't hitting on them. No one was looking at them like, "Oh, my God, there's a female." No one is thinking about sex. You get the job done with females there and with gays. You have people saying, "Oh, it's going to be distracting, ruin unit cohesiveness, just destroy the unit." Or they say because we are gay, we are too sensitive. We are already there, and there are more of us than you think. There are at least a couple of gay people in every unit, if not more. I'm talking from every rank, even lieutenants, generals, majors, captains.

* * *

When I got home, the talk of reenlistment came up. The intelligence people wanted me to go into their MOS.[2] It was a real cool job, and you even get to dress in civilian clothes. I agreed to do it. But I met a guy and started to have a relationship. He was in the military. He was an MP on base. He was getting out soon, and he was like, "It's not worth it being gay in the military." I didn't know what to do and decided to get out and not risk getting caught.

Two and a half months later, I was a wreck. I couldn't deal with anything. I couldn't function. I was lonely. We had broken up, and no one understood me. I was constantly in work mode. I couldn't sleep. I was by myself a lot, working the third shift at a convenience store for almost four months. A really good friend of mine, the first guy I came out to, wanted to know how things were going for me. He had gotten out, too, and things weren't going well for him, either. He said, "Why don't you move down here? At least we could help each other." I was there three months, and then he met a girl and moved out. I had an apartment to pay for on my Appleby's salary. I couldn't get a job that paid more than the minimum wage to save my life. No one wanted me. I tried every company, but they always hired within the company or someone's brother. I had these qualifications. I could listen to 19 radios, open up mail, and talk to my mother at the same time. I thought doing 911 would be the perfect job for me, but no one would hire me. To go from an extremely responsible job, giving these communications messages that were

---

[2]Military occupation specialty (job).

40

saving lives and making a difference, to "Would you like mashed potatoes or french fries with that?" It was hard. I had to lower my standards to work for a place like that, but I have to pay my bills.

I heard it takes 11 or 12 years to adapt to being home. I remember hearing that and laughing. Now, I believe it's true. You meet with your friends, and their whole thing is what are they going to do that night or on the weekend. I used to go and just sit at home. Our priorities were different. It was hard finding friends. People were boring to me, not that I was an exciting person. I didn't fit in anywhere. I thought they talked about stupid stuff.

So I felt I needed to get back in the Marine Corps. I started the paperwork and met with the recruiter, and he couldn't give me the jobs I wanted or in the time frame. A few weeks before I was scheduled to go back in, I went to Washington, D.C., with my boyfriend at the time. The Legal Service Defense Network—they help gays in the military—was having an event. I went to a seminar they had and told them that I was going in again, and they were shocked. They couldn't believe I came. They told me there were cameras there, and the military could find out, but I wanted to stay. I met a guy who was in for 19 years, 11 months, and two weeks, and he was an officer. He was kicked out two weeks before retirement because they found out he was gay. He was left with nothing—no pension, no pay, nothing. And he said it can and probably would happen to me if I reenlisted. I was shocked.

I got sick. Was I doing the right thing? Will this ruin my life? If you are dishonorably discharged, it can really mess you up. This guy had been in wars and had won medals, and he just couldn't even go to school because he couldn't pay for it. They took his GI Bill.

It made me very angry. I called my old boss and said I was thinking of going back in. He said he would take me back in a heartbeat, but he wanted to ask me a question. "Did you have relations when you were in the military?" I was like, "Did I have relations?" and I said, "With who?" And he said, "With other men?" and I said, "No, I did not." He then said, "The reason I ask is that there were rumors that you were gay and that when you were getting out, you were talking about it."

Before I got out, I had told more people, and they told more people, and it spread like wildfire, and it made it all the way to my boss. He was a great leader and a great guy, and we had a good relationship, and he liked my work. He said, "You can get back in, and you can work for me, but if I know, how many other people know? How long will it take before you don't work for me anymore? I'd hate to see that happen to you."

It was against the law for him to ask, but he did it because he cared. I didn't go back in.

* * *

I go to Montgomery County Community College. I've had about six majors, but now after I graduate, I want to go to the police academy.

While we were in Iraq, I was all for Bush. I stood behind him. I didn't see a problem with his decisions. He was our leader, the top of the food chain. I defended him to my parents. I told them that he knows what he is dong. But now that I'm home, I'm disgusted. I'm definitely patriotic. I hold America in a high regard. I hope that one day my freedoms are here, that I'll see them in my lifetime. I wake up every day with the hope that one day we can serve in the military, that one day we can get married, that one day it won't matter if you are gay. But if they lifted the ban, nothing will change. We are already serving. We are in Iraq right now.

KELLY DOUGHERTY

National Guard Sergeant
Lives: Colorado Springs, Colorado
Iraq War Service: February 2003–February 2004

I was naive. I thought I wouldn't be one of the people sent. I heard the drumbeats for war, but I thought my unit wouldn't be deployed. We were a medical unit and not a unit that went on the field. We did records and immunizations, but I was involuntarily transferred to my old military police unit and was told we were getting deployed the next day. The people in that unit knew for several weeks, but I found out the day before. I told them they didn't want me. I'm in school, and I'm against the war. It sounds stupid, but I went there and I told them that. My commander said it doesn't matter. I was conflicted, and I didn't know if I should refuse to go and suffer the consequences, which would have meant being brought up on a court-martial or leaving the country. I thought about getting pregnant or smoking a bunch of pot, but the alternatives were not that great. By the time I got my wits together, I was in Kuwait.

I was stationed at a port doing base security during the initial part of the war. There were a lot of alarms going off because of the Scud missiles being fired at us. You'd get into your gear and go into a concrete bunker and hope our guys shoot them down before they hit us. I never believed the Iraqis had the chemical weapons, but part of me was unsure because they kept telling us they did. It was really scary.

You'd try to take a shower real quick, but it always happened that when you would add the shampoo in your hair, that's when the alarm would go off. One time it had been a really long day, and alarms were going off constantly. It was nighttime, and as I was falling asleep, the whole ground shook. The windows blew out, and I think the part that was really scary was looking around seeing the faces of the other people, of the officers, and seeing how freaked out they were and how they could not control the panic.

I thought about it later and thought how many American bombs and missiles landed in people's neighborhood and what that must have been like. It happening to us one time sent everyone into a tailspin, and there was such disorder. For it to happen to the Iraqis day after day after day, it must have been terrible.

We didn't trust our higher-ups to keep us safe. It seemed at the time the top leaders' goals were to get us far into Iraq and put us into as much shit as they could. That way they could say, "We were in Baghdad, caught terrorists, and were in firefights." They could come back with the glory of their unit being hard-core. With my unit, there were no strong bonds of loyalty and trust.

An Egyptian man who worked for one of the contractors said he was upset with the war and then drove his pickup truck through a crowd of soldiers who were in line for something. One of our soldiers shot him, and the man was seriously wounded. My best friend was standing in line and saw it all happen, and it was really chaotic. I thought a missile was coming in because of all the commotion.

My friend Elizabeth ran to me and said, "Don't freak out. Don't freak out." And I'm like, "What happened?" Everyone had been shouting that we were under attack. It's hard to know the truth. In reality, one guy was driving, and one guy shot him in a front of a bunch of people.

There were so many weird rumors, like Iraqis had apples they were going to give to the soldiers, but some dogs ate them, and they were poisoned and died. It was very Snow White. Another story I heard was 30 marines went blind because they drank Iraqi moonshine. It was so absurd—30 blind marines and a barrel of poison apples.

*　*　*

The terrain was so flat. The ground is hard. The sand is so fine, like baby powder, and you couldn't understand how the people who lived out there made a living. They seemed to be planting something, but you couldn't see anything. They were so poor, they had no shoes and lived in mud and brick houses falling apart. When we patrolled further north, you'd see the houses blown in half by our bombs. Everything was destroyed and couldn't be rebuilt. When we left, it was the same. Our base is where we saw the progress. From no toilets and sleeping in tents in the beginning, to air-conditioned tents with wooden floors, Burger King, a huge PX,[1] all kinds of food and souvenirs made in India and China by the time we left. I also saw some walls being built around other countries' headquarters. The only progress I saw was in keeping the occupation.

*　*　*

We escorted convoys that were usually fuel tankers to supply the military. Meanwhile, there were long lines at Iraqi fuel stations that people would line up on all day. We'd also do patrols

---

[1] A large store on a military base selling groceries and other items, for exclusive military use.

to make sure that everything was OK and the route was clear. It seemed like most of the time, we were guarding ourselves. If we didn't have enemies, we were quickly making them. Fuel tankers would break down or get a flat tire. Iraqi men and boys would try and get something out of the disabled truck, and we would be called to guard the vehicle. So we could be guarding the vehicle for hours while we waited for the contractor. It never failed that 99 percent of the time, after trying to keep back a hundred Iraqis, we were told to leave the vehicles or else to burn them. This is after shooting the Iraqis with mace and rubber bullets to keep them away from it. We would then burn it right in front of them. I was ashamed. I didn't even want to look at the Iraqis. I was part of the destruction and unnecessary violence. I didn't want to do it, but there was nothing I could say to them. It was very frustrating to know that our job was to piss off the Iraqis, but it was either destroy the vehicle or else. The Iraqis wanted to tear off the metal doors and take off the tires and whatever else they could salvage. You'd see shops they set up at the side of the road with tires and junk. They had so little that anything we had would have value. But the theory was that if we gave it to them, then they would know they could have it. It was like they were two-year-old children you needed to punish. They were worried that if we let the Iraqis have it, they would try and run trucks off the road, which they were trying to do anyway.

I mostly guarded oil tankers, but one time I was guarding a truck that was filled with water. And right in front of the base, a pallet fell out of the truck, while a bunch of Iraqis watched. Instead of just letting them have the water, the humvees ran over the water over and over again, smashing the bottles and what they missed, they picked up, opened, took a sip, and then dumped it on the ground.

The Iraqis can't afford bottled water, and lot of the water they have is contaminated. The humvees couldn't pick the pallet up, so the logical thing you would think is to take as much as you can and leave the rest there for the Iraqis. The same guys who ran over the water were the same ones you'd see go in an orphanage and give out care packages. Then they'd feel really good because they are helping.

One day they do something great; the next day it's totally different. The most I can say is we gave candy to their kids. "Sorry we blew up your neighborhood and killed your father, but here is some candy."

We did house raids, but by the time we got there, all the men had left, and only the women and children were there. So either they screamed, cried, or stood silently. There were times we took women into the police station because the men were not there, and from what I know from their culture, it's a huge disgrace to do that to their women. We had a way we wanted to do things, and the Iraqi people had a completely different way of doing things. Americans in general think our way is the best way, and if you don't do it our way, you are stupid.

The majority of my unit wanted to help, but there was nothing we could do to overcome the damage. We were out there doing these patrols, and we didn't have translators if something were to go wrong. If there were insurgents or we pulled a car over, we could communicate with them only with what little English they knew and the pantomimes we could do. At the end, we got translators.

Our last mission was to help train Iraqi highway patrol, which made sense, but it was only for a month. One of the big things they keep saying is we need to train Iraqi security forces, but a lot of people hate the police force because there are no other jobs, and they are afraid for anyone to know they have joined. So the police asked us if we could get them a mask and face cover so people wouldn't know who they were. When we were training the highway patrol, we did these road blocks. Just imagine that if you're trying to go to the bank or your son's house, and there is this foreign military telling you to get out of your car and searching you and your car. It's very humiliating, and we would search the women, too, because they might have a gun or bomb. But in their culture, you can't touch a woman who is not your wife, and they would get upset. There was a lot of misunderstanding. What we are doing now is racist and goes beyond that. It's like they can't take care of themselves. The only way to live is how we tell them to because they are not capable of doing it themselves. They are too uneducated, savage, and poor. That feeling really permeates the military. I saw people who I liked in my own unit, who I respected, treat the Iraqis so bad and say they are so stupid, dirty, and disgusting. To hear people say those things, talk about the Iraqis like they were nothing, and feel such a hatred for them was very upsetting. Even myself at times, I would say that I hated the Iraqis. You are so overwhelmed, and it seems like they are there to take out your frustrations. It's really confusing.

There is no right or wrong there. There is no defined end goal. Democracy in place is not a realistic goal. It doesn't make sense and can't be possible if we are occupying them, and plus you have all the lies going into it. We know that the weapons never existed, but most American people don't care. They care more about who will be the next member of INXS than that. I wanted to talk to the Iraqi people. I wanted to talk to the women. How absurd would that be: "Hi, I have three weapons on me that could kill you, but, hey, let's talk woman to woman." In the beginning, some would wave, but after a while, it was less than that.

I did get a two-week leave, and all I wanted was to go back and never return, but I knew I had to go back, and so I tried not to think about it. So there I was, going to Macy's shopping for shoes, eating in nice restaurants. But in two weeks, I knew I'd be back in the desert in a humvee with three guns.

My father didn't want me to go back. My father wanted to kidnap me. He had me talk to a lawyer and go over my options, but I knew that I was going back. I knew it was almost over, and I didn't want to put myself through this just to refuse to go back. I knew my best friend was there, and she made it bearable. I couldn't abandon her. I thought wouldn't it be ironic if I went back for the last few months of my tour and got killed.

When we finally came home for good, I had been there a long time, and I thought it would be great, but it was not so great to be home.

You go in your house, and it's all the same, and you see your friends and you say, "I was just in Iraq for a year," and they say, "What was it like?" And you say, "It sucked." But you look in their eyes, and you see they don't want to hear it. So you stop talking to people. It was hard to relate to people that I'd been through such a huge experience, and it had a huge effect on thousands of lives instantly and so many more through the association. I didn't understand why everyone didn't care about this war.

I had a boyfriend, and we stayed together while I was gone. But when I got home, my boyfriend would say, "Yeah, it's bullshit, but what can I do about it?" We broke up.

My mom was like, "I support you, and I'm proud of you." Then she voted for Bush. How could you vote for someone who tried to kill me? She would have been one of those people who say, "My daughter died for a good cause." But I would want her to be like Cindy Sheehan[2] and say, "What the fuck?" She believes she supports me to the fullest extent, but I can't reconcile that. How could she support me and a president who is doing such horrible things? So we don't talk about it.

There was also the part of me that did so many weird things that I didn't want to tell people. They'd look at you in different way, especially people you are close to. I couldn't tell people that when I was in Iraq, I was laying on a flatbed truck waiting for hijackers so we could shoot them. Or that I hit people with bayonets so that I could get them away from me.

---

[2]Sheehan is an antiwar leader whose son was killed in the Iraq War.

I think we should pull out the troops. What we are doing now is not working. If this war is based on lies, why are we there? Why are U.S. soldiers being killed? Why are soldiers back for a third time? I have a friend who can't sleep; families have fallen apart; vets can't find jobs. All of this is because they were used as pawns in this war. I don't think we can fix it by staying.

GERALD DUPRIS

Army Specialist

Lives: Cheyenne Reservation, Eagle Butte, South Dakota

Iraq War Service: November 2002–August 2003

I come from a long line of veterans who fought for their country. My grandfather served in World War II, my father and many uncles in Vietnam, my sister in Bosnia, many cousins in Desert Storm, a cousin in Afghanistan, and I was in Iraq.

There is nothing here in the reservation. That's why I wound up in the army. I was walking to the store for my grandmother one day when all of a sudden, an army recruiter in a white Jeep pulled up next to me and said, "How old are you?" I said I was 17 years old and that I would be 18 in December. He said, "Have you ever thought about joining the military?" I told him it never crossed my mind. He took my name and information and then sent me a video and brochures about the army and the military police. It was pretty cool what the MPs did. One thing led to another, and I decided that was what I wanted to do. I was tired of school. I didn't want to go to college. The military sounded fun and was a chance to see the world. There isn't much to do back home. There's a lot of unemployment. So I wanted to be an MP, but there weren't any slots available, and so I became a tank mechanic.

After 9/11, there was deployment after deployment. We were sent to Kuwait a couple of days before Thanksgiving in 2002. We were supposed to go for six months and then come home to see our family. Four months passed, and then at the end of March, they told us that orders came down and that we were going to go to the Iraqi border and to wait there until the orders came to go across. So we just sat there and got everything ready in the middle of nowhere with no electricity and running water. We lived in tents.

Then we got the order to go into Iraq. We were supposed to clear a road so companies can go through. So we are driving, and the first thing I remember is hearing this whizzing noise, and I turn and see a bunch of Iraqi troops running around with AK-47s, and I'm like, "Oh, my God, what did I get myself into? I'm only 19 years old, and what am I going to do? This is crazy." A lot of things are running through my head. I'm wondering what my family is thinking. I started thinking of home and told myself, "Don't break down," "Don't cry," and "Don't get scared." A few times I felt like crying but did not let myself break down. Once we started laying fire at them, they threw their weapons in the air and started running. This one guy was running; he was just stripping off his clothing, his uniform, as if he didn't want to be known as an Iraqi soldier. After that, they told us we are no longer tank mechanics. It was time to bring out the infantry inside of us.

We had to hit every town on the way up. The towns looked like ghost towns. Everyone was in their homes. People peeked out, scared. There were lots of firefights. But there was a lady and her family, her children sitting in front of their house drinking and eating while all this shooting and fighting was going on. That's a picture I remember. How could someone be so relaxed when a war was going on? They were drinking tea, eating food. This lady even came over and offered us some food, but we couldn't take it. She could be a decoy; it could be poisoned.

The Iraqis are very friendly people, but at the same time, they are corrupt. They can make a lie sound good. "Oh, no, I never shot anyone," they'd say. A few days later, you'd see that same person in a firefight against us. One of the interpreters could be someone who fought against us. I didn't really trust them. We asked where they were hiding the weapons, and the Iraqis didn't want to say anything because Saddam was still loose. The people were very scared. We told them they had nothing to fear unless they hurt us. We were nice to them. If we had a dollar in our pocket, we would give it to them so they could feed their family for a few weeks because our currency was more valuable than theirs. Our dollar was gold to them. Give them $10 and they were rich. They could buy a car with that.

We went to a man-made lake called Lake Saddam. It was made for him. People used to live there, and he just dredged it to have his own personal swimming area. These Iraqi kids bought inner tubes, and we took them out there. The kids' dad was with them, and he said, "I used to live right around here, me and my mother; that's where we used to live, but when they flooded us out, we had to move."

* * *

On May 1, 2003, the president told the nation that the war was over, that fighting would cease, but it never stopped. We always knew it was far from over. We still had land mines and RPGs [rocket-propelled grenades], firefights and patrols. We had many things to deal with all the time.

They told us many times we were going home, but it didn't happen. Guys got real upset. Me, I just went back to the bunk, grabbed my headphones and grabbed my drawing pad, and started drawing things of home. That's how much I missed it. I drew the horses, prairie, the buffalo, the plains, farms, and cornfields. That's what I wanted to see so bad instead of sand and

135-degree heat. I didn't want to see or feel that anymore. I hate sand. I didn't want to see mud houses. I didn't want to see Iraq anymore.

Finally, after almost a year, they told us we were going home, and this time it was for real. After a couple more delays, we made it home. When we made our final approach to Maine, everyone started screaming. We were so happy. When we landed, there was a line of Korean and Vietnam veterans to greet us. I just remember seeing old men and women waiting to shake our hands and tell us we were good men and women and we deserved to be home. It was the best welcome home I ever got.

I remember this one guy, a Korean War veteran, who said, "Thank you for what you did. I've been in a war. I know what you've been through." I said, "I am just happy I'm still alive." We grabbed a cup of coffee. Most of the guys went to the bar because drinks were on the house. But I sat down with this Korean War vet, and we talked. He told me about his experiences, and I told him about mine, and it felt good. It felt good to talk to someone who's been through a war. His last name was Walker, and he was a navy Seabee. He told men "You go home and join your family and enjoy the rest of your life because you have done good. You did something great. Don't let anyone ever bring you down because you did something great." He made me feel proud.

When we got back to our base, we had to get mental health help for about a week. That really helped me because I had some problems. Then, they gave us a 30-day leave.

I remember jumping on that plane back home but kind of tricking my family. I let everyone off the plane first, then I peeked around the corner and saw them all. So I got my video camera and started videotaping them and walking toward them. They were like, "Is that him? Is that him?"

I was a lot skinnier. I weighed 198 when I left, but when I came back I weighed 158 pounds. I lost a lot of weight. They finally recognized me, and we hugged. My mother was crying.

I took them all out to eat, then went home to Eagle Butte. They had another welcome home for me there on the rez [reservation]. They made me walk down Main Street, which is something the Cheyenne do for all the soldiers who live on the reservation. Eagle Butte is a little town. But they had drummers, and the Lakota warriors marched carrying the Cheyenne flag, American flags, South Dakota flag, and the POW flag. There were drummers, fire, ceremonial celebration, and a lot of people came out to watch.

They also put your name on yellow ribbons and put it on a big tree we call the "Support Tree." In the celebration, you walk up to tree and take your name off. There are a lot of names on that tree.

It all really felt good. All my friends were there. I hadn't seen them in a year and a half. They came out, gave me a hug, and shook my hand. I love the people back home who supported me. I have a list of the names of people who wrote to me, who sent me newspapers and pictures just so I could feel at home when I was over there. When I was in Iraq and saw a soldier die, I thought of the people back home. Instead of us being there in Iraq, the war could have happened here.

After I went back to base, the army tried to keep me there involuntarily. I signed up for three years, and they wanted to keep me indefinitely. But it didn't happen. I got out June 10, 2004.

When I got home, I just wanted to stay home. A lot of people didn't reenlist. I wanted to, but it was, like, fuck it. I didn't want to go back to Iraq. It makes me mad thinking about all those people I killed for this war that doesn't have a meaning. I probably killed about 250 people, but the confirmed kills are the ones you see, the ones the army credits you for. I have seven confirmed kills, but I shot a lot of people, and I just know they didn't survive.

After more than a year back from Iraq, I have my own family. My girlfriend and I have a daughter. I have thought about signing back up, but now I've got this job. I am a Cheyenne River law enforcement officer. I just started that job last week, and within one week, I put in 60 hours, 8 A.M. to 8 P.M. It's just a job that most people don't like or want, but it pays good money. A military background is supposed to help to have priority in jobs, but it took eight months before I got this job. Before that, I did babysitting and I worked at a bar. I got this job because no one wanted it.

* * *

Now, I tell a lot people I want to go back in the army. The army is better than being at home. I am happy now with my girlfriend, but we want something different than the rez. The military is the best thing because you get to go different places. We can move anywhere. I just want the best thing for my family. I put them first before myself. Right now, my division is back in Iraq for its second rotation. Had I stayed in, I would be back there for a year or more. A year there, and I'd probably go crazy. When all this Iraq War stuff ends, maybe then I'll go back.

Jon Soltz

Army Captain
Lives: Pittsburgh, Pennsylvania
Iraq War Service: May 2003–September 2003

I've always wanted to be in the military. When I was 16, I had a heart defect, and my dad sent me to Israel for two months. Everyone there had to serve in the military. All their leaders had served in the military. I felt that I should be in the military, too, but I wasn't able-bodied. But then I got my heart fixed by this new kind of surgery. All of a sudden I could be in the military. In Israel it's a rite of passage, so it became my rite of passage.

When I went to college, I signed up for ROTC. I also did it because I felt American people don't serve. It's something you do because you can't get into college. It's like, "My kid is not going to go in the military. It's for the kid down the street because he is not as good as my son or daughter." That's not right. The people in the military are the people that are protecting the stockbrokers and lawyers. These are the people protecting your sons and daughters. America has given everyone the opportunity to be born in a hospital, to have basic medicine, to have freedom of speech, to have a guarantee of rights and liberties.

I was excited about going to war. I was ready. I was going to be a piece of American history. I was so cocky. I kept thinking, "What is France going to do when they find the weapons?" In my heart, I thought the weapons of mass destruction were there.

I got to Kuwait, and we had not one piece of armored equipment. We only had some body armor. I wanted to be the first to lead the convoy into Iraq, and I jumped right in. We had one mission: to push the battalion to Iraq. It was one of the most physically demanding things you can do. It was so hot, our water was boiling. You couldn't drink it. The president was soon going to declare the war was over, and leadership wanted the combat patches, so if we didn't get to Iraq before the president spoke, then the war would be over, and we wouldn't get a patch.

We left at 0500. We drove all day and night. At our release point, a military police unit from the National Guard joined us and took us and was to take us to where we were going to be stationed, LSA Dogwood. As we were driving, there was an ordnance [bomb] on the ground, so they rerouted us, and we were exhausted. Next thing I know, we were in an ambush. We had RPG [rocket-propelled grenade] and small arms fire coming at us, and we couldn't speed up because the escort in front of us wasn't. It caused a Slinky effect. We were on a road we shouldn't have been on. We were lucky no one was hurt. I was like, "Wow, I guess the war was not over." It was the best thing that happened to us. It let everyone know we were still at war.

So we set up base in what looked like a dustbowl. Now that area is called the "Triangle of Death," but we didn't know that. We had no air conditioners or port-o-potties. We had no e-mail or phones. We were completely out of touch. I felt very disconnected. It was hard.

Our job was support operations for the First Armored Division out of the Baghdad Airport and LSA Dogwood.

We figured out we should move our supplies from where we were because we were going to have soldiers at Baghdad Airport and the four area divisionals. We had no e-mail or phones. We were completely out of touch. It was difficult.

From our base, we were running a convoy a day to Baghdad and back. I was concerned with the logistical parts of things. I needed to get food, medical supplies, and everything you need to support a unit. Let me tell you, providing support ops [operations] in Iraq is very dangerous. We didn't realize what was ahead. We did this a couple of weeks with no major incidents. I remember the colonel saying, "One of these days someone is going to die."

We were in a meeting one morning, and a fuel convoy I sent called back to our headquarters and said they had been in an ambush. One of my men was killed—Smith. He was the nicest soldier. A piece of shrapnel went in the back of his head and into his brain. Smith was driving a fuel truck, and there was a bomb, an IED [improvised explosive device], on the side of the road. He was not in an armored vehicle. His mom has since come out against the president. She said her son loved the army but didn't like the war. I read in the paper that when his mom heard that, she went ballistic. I can't blame her. Her son died in a convoy that I sent. The failure came from the highest level, the political level. He didn't have the right equipment to survive—none of us did. We did the best we could with the equipment we had. The only one who could have made a difference was the president.

From then on, we collected all the body armor, and anyone who left the base had to wear it. We even found some Iraqi body armor we used because we didn't have enough for our soldiers.

Everything just got worse from there. We didn't have the right equipment. We had an insurgency going on, and America didn't realize we were still at war. The next week, another one of our vehicles exploded, but no one died, but all that was left was a burning truck. After that, we started getting hit all the time. The news of dead soldiers spread fast.

I wound up getting transferred to Baghdad Airport. There were more casualties. We were getting mortared all the time. I was exhausted. I got sick with sand fly fever and had a fever of 104. I lost 20 pounds. It was so hot, like having a hairdryer in your face all the time. I worked there for about seven weeks. Finally, it came time for me to leave. I had nothing left.

When I left Iraq and went back to Germany, that is the day the war started for me. That's the day I had to start living with it for the rest of my life. I was ready to go back to Pittsburgh and surprise my girlfriend, but I soon heard from a friend that she had left me for another guy. I couldn't sleep or eat. I loved her. I was already in bad shape because of everything that happened to me in Iraq that I didn't get to talk about. I had packaged it all up in a part of my body and hadn't dealt with any of it. I was pretty destroyed. I started reeling. I had other problems. They told me a soldier I knew, a good friend, had gotten blown up in a daisy chain that went off in his face. I went to go see him, and he was there with his fiancée. Shrapnel had hit his face everywhere. His arm was shattered. It hurt me so much to see him like that. I didn't cry in Iraq, but I cried when I looked at him. I don't know, I looked at this guy and said, "I just hope that this is worth it because you paid the price." That's a question no American soldier should have to ask.

Then I started having more problems. People I knew started dying, and I started having these dreams that I was getting mortared. The mortar would get closer and closer, and then it would get on top of you, and you'd wake up. That's the way it went for months. Things were getting worse in the news. I was lucky I wasn't there, but my mind was messed up. I had no idea what I was going to do. I was completely in a depressed state. For two months there was nothing to do at work because I was getting out. I just hung out in Germany. Then I went home to the States, and it got worse because now I was around people who didn't understand me at all. How many 26-year-olds can deal with this? I went to live with one of my friends. One day he came home after he had been drinking, and I was asleep. He screamed, "Mortars!" I freaked out and said, "Don't ever do that to me again." After a month, I couldn't take it and went to live with another friend.

I started graduate school, but I was only going to take one class because I couldn't concentrate. I couldn't even watch movies. The lady at the University of Pittsburgh told me if I went full-time, they would give me the money. So I started doing three classes. I began to study the war and write using my experiences on the ground.

Iraq is probably the most misunderstood war America has ever fought. What we found in Iraq were not weapons of mass destruction but a bunch of people who were brutalized. My professor asked me to give a presentation to the class. In my uniform, I told one of my classes that the war was poorly planned and that we have no allies and not enough troops allocated. I ended my presentation with a picture of my kid, Smith, who was killed in Iraq and said, "That's the price of the war in Iraq." I won them over. But I was so sick. I was crashing. I wrote this paper on Iraq and e-mailed it to everyone I knew because I didn't want to talk about it. Meanwhile, I am having dreams that I killed four people. I couldn't relate to anyone my age. I didn't know anyone who had been to Iraq no one understood me. I was convinced I had PTSD [posttraumatic stress disorder]. I couldn't concentrate.

I was exhausted when I walked into the VA hospital in Highland Park. The nurse said, "What's wrong with you?" And I said, "I'm exhausted. I'm not the same person." I was crying. I told her I was having nightmares. She told me I was articulate. She said I should talk to other soldiers who came back from Iraq. I can't tell you how much it meant to me. Her name is Mary Anne Meador, and she helped me a lot. She is still my friend.

Then I get this phone call from this guy, a Vietnam veteran, who said he was calling on behalf of Senator John Kerry. I said I didn't like when Kerry voted down the $87 billion appropriations for the soldiers because those soldiers needed it. I don't care if he was for the war or not, but we needed that stuff. But I wanted to help John Kerry. Kerry's been to war. He said he would give me five minutes with Kerry.

I met him at the airport. I wasn't nervous. I looked him in the eye and said, "American soldiers need your help." I told him what was going on about how overextended the army was and how we had no armor. He said he was going to call me, and he did. He said, "When I came back from Vietnam, I was just like you. I was angry because I felt like I wasn't told the truth."

I told him, "I'm the guy that went to Iraq with no armored vehicles. I'm the guy that went to Iraq that was ambushed the first time he drove in. I'm the guy who after one of my men died, I heard my commander in chief say, 'Bring it on.' I'm the guy who looked my friend and fellow soldier in the face when he was blown up in the hospital and asked, 'Is it worth it?' That's a question no soldier should have to ask. I'm the guy who got help at a VA hospital, and my commander said he is going to close that hospital."

I never thought I would get five minutes with him, and now I was part of his team. He was the first person to get through to me to let me know that what I was feeling was OK. I became Kerry's Pennsylvania veterans coordinator.

I've spent the last year on active duty again training troops at Fort Dix. I'm giving back to the troops. It helps me a lot knowing I'm giving back. At this point, it doesn't matter whether I'm for or against the war because these troops are going out to Iraq, and I train them hard every day. I will work them superhard as long as the war doesn't end. My next step after this is to get involved in the political debate and push as hard as I can for a viable exit strategy.

People who say that we should leave right now just don't understand what is going on, and the Far Right is crazy if they think I'm going to accept some bullshit like the "stay the course forever" argument. We need an honest political debate on benchmarks. The insurgency will wait us out 2 years or 10. The policymakers should have thought long and hard about what was going to happen in Iraq after the American army leaves.

The men that got us in this war are the men who did not go to Vietnam, who did not serve when they had their chance. They turned their backs on America and have now turned into the greatest war hawks in American history.

LISA HAYNES

Army Reserves Sergeant
Lives: Boynton, Oklahoma
Iraq War Service: April 2003–April 2004

I don't regret anything I have done in the service. I felt I was accomplishing something. I felt proud. It's just my last experience in Iraq—I know what a toll it has taken on me, and I can't take that back. The experiences I have had in the last two years have bought me down, but hopefully I'll get stronger. I just got to get there.

I joined the Army Reserves right out of high school in 1984, for the money. It wasn't a lot of money, but I thought it was. I wanted to do something different. I was from a small town, real small, Boynton, Oklahoma. It's an all-black town, of about 300-something people. I wanted to see other places. I wanted to travel, so I joined.

I did a lot of tours of three months and six months in my time. I worked in supply.

When the war started, I thought we were safe because we were a small unit. We helped in Desert Storm Stateside, shipping supplies. I thought we would do the same thing. I did not think a whole lot about it. I knew what I had to do, and I wasn't sweating it out. I knew there would always be a chance that we would be called up, and we were.

First we went to Lawton, Oklahoma, to get trained on what we were fixing to walk into. It was scary. I was a little anxious. I was getting into something, and I didn't have a clue as to what it was. We practiced the worst scenarios. I was a wife and mother. I have two teenage sons. They were big boys, but they were scared for me. I told them it would be OK, that this was just part of life. They understood and were supportive.

When I first got to Kuwait, the first thing they said was, "Welcome to the war." We got on buses. It was dark, flashlights everywhere. I was ready to do anything because it had to get done. That's when it got scary, not knowing what was going to happen. We slept in a big ol' tent. It took about a month to get used to the climate. It got up over 147 degrees. It was hot all the time. I was on the first group that went to Iraq. We were split up. I got to Iraq on Saddam's birthday.

It was a hard trip. Just the different scenario you would see from Kuwait to Iraq. You see a lot of camels, people, dead animals. These big spiders would attack the camels. They would attach to each other, nest on the camels backs, and then eat them alive until they dropped. On the road we saw a lot of Iraqi kids, poor kids, hungry, pretty kids, malnourished with big stomachs. We weren't supposed to give them anything. They would come up to our vehicles hungry, and we couldn't give them anything. It was kind of hard seeing the kids like that, but you had to be sharp and on guard all the time. That by itself is a stress, knowing how on guard you had to be and observant all the time, especially when you saw how hungry the kids were. You wanted to help them, but you couldn't.

It was scary, really scary. They'd tell you, "Get out of my city," "We hate you," or "We love you, we love." A lot of those people were angry that we're there taking over and invading their country. The majority of them were haters. You can't blame them because that was all that they knew. Everything we did was chancy, because we didn't know the type of people we were dealing with.

It took 24 hours for us to get where we needed to go. You saw military people everywhere. It was Saddam's birthday, and there was a lot of shooting going on around you. You saw only men and boys. I never saw the women, really. Only time I saw them, they were way out on the field working, or they were witch doctors, but it was always old women. The women were laborers.

I ate MREs [meals ready-to-eat] for about two months straight. It's not good and not good on an everyday basis, but that's all we had. I was working every day, 16, 17 hours a day. We set up camp, dug foxholes on the perimeter. Some of us immediately had to be on guard stations because they were already climbing over the walls. I was in supply, but my job changed dramatically. I had one magazine with at least 30 rounds in them, and that's a load. With everything else you have on you, like your bulletproof vest, which is heavy, knives, and whatever else you can carry, it's a load on you. Guard duty was long hours, and you could be attacked at any time. It wasn't about being a woman; it was about working together. These people were coming over the walls. They were hungry. They didn't know where Saddam was. Everything was burnt and torn up around us. They were angry with us. We'd torn up their cities. We had about 80 to 90 people a night attacking us.

I have shot at them. I think I missed. I could have hit them. I don't know. It makes you feel kind of sad. A grenade hit a buddy I was right next to. All the nerves in his arms were destroyed, and he was right next to me when it happened. I've seen a lot of dead bodies, and that kind of thing will stick with you for the rest of your life.

One time, two cars ahead of us, a car was hit with a grenade. The insurgents drove right up on the side of it and blew it up, and that stopped the rest of us. I jumped out of the car, and the insurgents were there, and everything was action from there. They were coming after me, and they were close to me. I started hitting them. I used my weapon, my hands. I beat them down. Everyone doesn't think just to kill. We do have a conscience. If we can get around it, we do. I was trying to prevent myself from shooting them. A lot of young people in the service say they want to kill them, but they don't realize they have to live with it. The war gives you a lot of mental problems. I know, because I have to live with it.

One time, I was on a night shift, and I told my soldiers not to burn trash anymore, because we were finding live rounds and bones from wars years ago. But one guy decided to do it anyway, and then we heard a firing sound. One of our soldiers got shot in the arm. It was a perfect example of why they told us not to do it. The sergeant major asked me who did this. I was wearing glasses, and the sergeant major said, "Take those fucking glasses off. Why was he burning trash when we directly told you they should not?" Your soldiers do things, and you have to take the hit for it. I got an Article 15[1] for it. You have some rights, but other times you have to take a licking and keep on ticking. I was angry, but it did no good.

We were always getting hit. They tried to hit our mess halls and things. We didn't know when we were going to get to eat. We had no showers and took baths out of our hard hats. There was no privacy. There were a lot of women there. It was a city to itself. You know, there were a lot of married men, but it's like nothing when you are over there. The rules went out the window. Everyone was cohabitating. The morale was low, and everyone was missing home. We thought we were only going to be there six months. It didn't matter when the president said, "Mission accomplished," because we were still there. Nothing changed. To make a call, you had to wait hours. You had to sneak around and urinate in a bottle. I hated the lack of privacy. Some of my soldiers were suicidal. They had no money in their accounts, and their wives done left them. I had to talk them out of it. I had to be their counselor and their friend. Morale is down, and you are wondering what you are there for.

---

[1]Nonjudicial punishment that a commanding officer or officer in charge can award to members of his or her command for minor disciplinary offenses.

I was on the road when they killed Saddam's sons. I saw a lot of dead bodies then. We stopped when we saw this one guy. He had six, seven gunshot wounds, and when you are thrown out of a car, it is so much worse. His face, everything, was messed up. We called it in, but there was nothing they could do. That body laid out there for two days. When they did move it, they just pushed it to the side of the road. When we drove back, we saw it again. The hand had risen from rigor mortis. The body was swelling. That kind of stuff puts your mind in a strange place.

* * *

When I got home, it took them just a few days to release us. I felt they just wanted to get us off the money. They wanted to ship us all to the VA instead of seeing us and dealing with what our problems were.

When I came home, I wasn't aware of how I was acting. I didn't see it coming. I knew I was hurting in the back still. I was in a humvee accident in Iraq. I was in the backseat, and after we got hit, my hard hat flew down the road. I was in the hospital there for eight days. My feet were bad because I was in shoes 15, 16 hours a day. I knew that I was close to having my 20 years and knew that I was going to retire. I was ready to get out. It was half of my life. I'm 40 now. It was a hard thing to go through. I just made my E-6 [sergeant], and I would have stayed in longer if I wasn't hurt.

I started having flashbacks and hot and cold flashes. Any foreign people of color irritated me. What I went through started coming back to me. I was distant from people. I didn't want to be around people. I was real quiet. I was twitching, and I was hurting on top of that, which made me sad and depressed. I wanted to be seen by the medical board while I was still on active duty, and I had to fight to stay on active duty until they saw me. Once they did, everything was a slow process. I started seeing a counselor and realized it wasn't unusual what I was going through. The medical board found me unfit to serve. I couldn't do the push-ups, sit-ups, and couldn't lift the weight. They said if you were hurt, they would pay you half of your retirement money now instead of waiting until you are 62. I think only 2 of us out of 100 got that. They messed over a lot of reservist and National Guard people. They didn't want to pay us.

I was lucky, because there were so many elements to my injury that they gave me 30 percent disability and then said the VA would take care of the rest in the long run. Later they moved it up to 80 percent. I just had surgery on my knee.

You know, if I could just be like the way I was, that's all I want, not money. Nothing is worth what I have been through. I'd rather have my life back than use the system. I just want my life back. It's messed up my life to the point that I can't gather with people. I don't like groups. I can't ride horses and things I used to do. It's turned my life upside down. I am depressed a lot and crying a lot. I am so tired. My kids can't play with me the way they used to. I actually hit one of my sons because he tried to scare me. He came up behind me and said, "Boo," and my reflexes hit him. I tried to talk to them and tell them I am a very different person. I asked them to be patient with me. I'm moody, crying a lot, and I'm distant. I have a lack of motivation. I procrastinate. I hate it with a passion, but I've gotten so slow, and I forget stuff, and it frustrates me. In my job, I work at the VA as the head of the laundry, but my mind don't function the same. I used to love my job, but now it's so different. It's like I hate going to work. I hate going anywhere.

I wasn't like this when I went. When I was there, I did good, but it's like when I came back, everything just fell apart. Over there, I couldn't show a weak side. I had subordinates under me. I had to be in control. But once I got back, now my feelings can easily be hurt. I've been to depression classes and anger management. I see a counselor. I'm not in shape, I'm flabby, and I think it's triggered early menopause. I get upset and my heart races. I cry so much and get stressed-out so much. I just hurt. I can't even breathe. I sometimes can't stop myself from crying. I saw soldiers with no arms and their legs blown off, babies malnourished and hungry. I saw a lot of violence. I know that's part of war, but that doesn't make it easy.

My life is totally different and I can't adapt. My family at times makes me feel guilty because I always say that I don't want to do things. I haven't been shopping since I've been back. I don't even look at the news. I lived that. I don't want to see it. But when I was there, I didn't understand why we were there. I don't understand why we are still there, and a lot of soldiers feel the same way. All we know is what we were ordered to. We went with what we had to go with.

I never regretted anything I have done in the service until this last war. I felt like I accomplished something, and I was proud. I can't take anything back, but right now, it just has me down.

BEN FLANDERS

National Guard Sergeant

Lives: Danvers, Massachusetts

Iraq War Service: March 2004–April 2005

I was getting married on January 11, 2004. On December 22, 2003, I got a call from my chain of command at the National Guard, and they read what felt like a script: "Specialist Flanders, you are hereby ordered into active duty."

When I got the call, I was just about to go home. My fiancée and I were going to buy a bed for our new apartment, and I got the word that I needed to be in the armory on January 5. It was two days before Christmas Eve, and we were getting married in New Jersey, so whatever we had to do we needed to do it fast. I started thinking about what I was going to say to my fiancée and how I would hug her and give her a kiss on the forehead and tell her. I thought I would be brave about it. So I'm walking up the stairs heading to my apartment, and my legs are feeling heavy. I open the door, and she is cooking dinner. She wanted us out the door to get to the store, and it struck me that I was going to change our lives with what I had to say, and I was completely overwhelmed. I started crying and couldn't get it out for a couple of minutes. She was like, "What did you do?" Through my blubbering, I spit it out. So we sat down together and cried. The next day, we beelined it to New Jersey. We made phone calls that night to my mother and family members, and everyone was pretty shocked.

We got married two days after Christmas. We went down to New Jersey on December 23 and went to see a judge. We assembled everything together the best we could. We got married in a small wedding and had a reception in the basement of a church. It was a potluck kind of thing. Originally, we had planned to rent out a restaurant, and it was going to be catered.

The wedding also served as a good-bye. I didn't know if I'd see my family again. It really overshadowed the wedding. It was a very emotional service for everyone. It was joyous, but there was lots of anxiety. I spent three weeks with my wife while doing training in Manchester, New Hampshire. We did not have too much time together, and before we got married, we didn't live together. We had the honeymoon set up, but everything changed.

I couldn't leave the military even though my tour of duty was over. It ended in the fall of 2003. Rather than let you go, they have a stop-loss policy,[1] which is not ideal, but it is sound policy. It keeps the most qualified and trained personnel you can. My attitude was "This is what I'm asked to do." I didn't take too much time to complain about it. We had a mission. They didn't rewrite my contract. I was like, OK, fine. I wasn't the only guy extended under stop-loss.

We flew out to Kuwait on March 17, 2004, and got there one year after the initial invasion. That's when I got a preview in terms of living situation. Everyone was stuffed in a big tent, but in the more central part of the base, there were phone trailers with the Internet, a barber shop trailer, gift shop—interesting to see. It worked, and it made things easier. So we were in Kuwait for 10 days, and I found out we would be stationed in Anaconda. It's this huge hub, which

---

[1] A military policy that allows contracts to be extended during wartime.

would bring in cargo and airplanes. It housed a lot of the civilian guys, about 25,000. I said I did not care what we do except for convoy operations, because they were so vulnerable to attacks. Then, it turns out, that is exactly what we would be doing.

Kellogg Brown & Root were civilian contractors who were on the base. They ran the laundries, the PX,[2] and it was great, but it was at a cost. If you wanted a café, we would escort it to the base, and we would have to escort them through a dangerous part of Iraq. When you were the one escorting the damn stuff, it was crazy. We are risking our lives for that. We guarded ice, which is frozen water. You just didn't want to know what you were escorting. We got ambushed. We had amputees; some guys got shot in the head and died protecting supplies.

We had two primary tasks: convoy security, which was taking the supplies through the heart of the country and Baghdad, and we also patrolled major roads we used for supply routes. We looked for bad guys and dealt with them.

We replaced a company that had armored humvees. Remember, by spring of 2004, roadside bombs were an issue. You needed a tank or up-armored humvee, and we got them. We lucked out. So you'd suit up for the day, get your briefing, and go out to your sector. We would coordinate with the convoys, do IED [improvised explosive device] sweeps, and hope you find the IED before it finds

---

[2]A store located on a military base for exclusive military use.

the convoys. While on convoy, you just try to get through the kill zone, but when you are on patrol, that is your job: to fight.

A lot of time, the enemy is just some paid thugs, local guys. Sometimes you would meet two guys who expend the ammo, and then that was it. Other times a series of IEDs would go off. They would daisy-chain it, rig the tips so it would explode on command. They would use garage door openers and car alarms to send the signals. You would be driving 50 miles an hour, as fast as you can. Iraq is dirty, but they have dumps on the side of the road where their cows graze. People would be living in these slums, and there was stuff everywhere. They said look for Pepsi cans or trash piles, which is where the IEDs would be, but there were cans everywhere, trash everywhere, and sometimes you'd see wires sticking out. We were hauling, going 50 miles an hour, but sometimes a driver would see it and stop. We'd pull over on and then call people to depose of it. You breathe that sigh of relief when you see it. When they go up, you see the big clouds of smoke, and your heart skips a beat. We did night operations and could hardly see them in the day. Imagine at night.

A couple of times in April and November, they invaded in larger numbers, and there was a series of coordinated attacks. There would be very intense fighting rather than a mixed bag of characters who'd shoot at us and head back into their houses. We would face 20 to 30 insurgents at a time, but we had radio. We could call attack helicopters, and the insurgents died by the dozens. They paid for it.

The Iraqis didn't have a great economy. They were living this kind of agricultural lifestyle. All their buildings were destroyed, but they were busy doing their thing. We would get looks sometimes, but people would wave, especially the kids. It basically was like nothing really happened, and suddenly, you would get in an ambush, and you're like, "Where did this come from?" We were confined mostly to the main roads and weren't allowed to go to the villages. We were segregated from the population. If we spotted an IED, we wouldn't let traffic go by. They would get out of their car, and they'd ask you if you had kids or a wife. They were curious.

The majority of the people in Iraq had things they did before the invasion and kept doing. We didn't reorder their society in all levels, not in an economic or lifestyle sense.

We helped out where we could. If there was a traffic jam, and I saw a taxi and there was a woman with a lot of children, I'd give them water. The insurgency didn't come from an Iraqi identity or a nationalistic impulse. They want to see us out, obviously. Anytime a foreign military is on their land isn't great, but it wasn't like Vietnam in the sense that a large group of people were fighting for a certain ideologue. The Iraqis just want to provide for their families and move from point A to point B. The majority doesn't agree with the violence. I had long conversations with our interpreter. He said people were sick of Saddam, and everyone was in fear and afraid. When the insurgents saw their opportunity, the pathway was already laid out for them to easily oppress and intimidate openly. We have no concept of this in America. Iraq is very economically stagnant. There are a lot of poor people, and it's easy to motivate them to rise up against the United States. Our company would stumble upon beheaded people as a way to intimidate them to be against the United States. Who are the good and the bad guys? You feel all you see is good guys. You see nice people at the market, not attacking us. But there are these little groups of people moving freely and causing this massive disruption on an international scale.

These guys in Iraq are fighting to keep democracy out of the picture and America from influencing any part of Iraq. Democracy could have been able to take root if it wasn't for this small group. It seems to me that they could have understood equality and justice, but they weren't given that chance. Insurgents took it away. But when they had a chance, they voted. The problem is the insurgents are overshadowing everything. They are winning in a sense. There is a moderate majority of Iraqis who are not extremist. We are trying to win their hearts and minds by providing them with a water treatment facilities, improving local jobs, putting in electrical grids, preserving their oil, and at the same time, insurgents are trying to win it by bombings, random killings, and assassinations. Which is more effective? I would say insurgents are more effective. They can hold sway over people more effectively.

* * *

I was really having a hard time. I was burned-out. You get sick of the grind, sick of the mission, all these IEDs, the casualty count. While I was there, 1,000 people died. This whole concept of death was so much clearer. At the convoy briefing, they tell you what was going on, and every day the whole report was circled red marking all the insurgent attacks.

My wife tried not to think about the danger. She was just missing me. I remember having a conversation with her, and she is crying, "I miss you, I miss you." I celebrated our first-year wedding anniversary in Iraq. We never talked about the danger I was in. All I was thinking about was the danger. I didn't know if the next day, I would be gone and not see her ever again. I had to contend with an imminent threat. It was an extremely stressful environment in Anaconda. It was prone to attacks. You were not safe on the inside or outside. I lived in constant dread. You never knew. We were lucky. We never had a death in our company, but we did have a number of serious injuries.

One of the serious injuries happened to a private on the base who was in front of the PX when a rocket hit the corner of it. He had shrapnel thorough his back. It shattered his right arm, and he was close to dying and had to have some serious surgery. Three people died in that attack. And about a dozen were injured. One of the other guys who died was hours away from going home. He was in the country for a year, and he was leaving, but the plane was delayed. He had just been on the Internet planning a romantic getaway with his wife and was meeting some guys at the PX to wait for their plane.

I was in Iraq for 11 months and one day and away from home for 14 months. I had a dramatic homecoming. It was euphoric. My unit was escorted by state police through New Hampshire to a hangar. All the families came out, 2,000-plus. They brought us in buses and erected this huge flag. As we were driving to the hangar, we saw this sea of people. Officials roped off a pathway for us so we could see our families.

A band was playing, and everyone was cheering. This was it. We were done—no more sacrifice, just pure enjoyment of surviving and being reunited with our families.

I reenlisted again. There was something profound about serving my country, and although I had been a national guardsman for six years and I was getting paid and getting benefits, I wasn't seeing where I was providing service for what I was getting until I was actually deployed and put my ass on the line. It really readjusted that whole focus that service to the country is really important. It transcended the mission that I was in. I realized it's important to have a strong military, and I also realized we need to keep our leaders accountable. Do I support the invasion? I'm not 100 percent sure. We need congressional hearings about what led to that.

I believe in this country. It needs people who are critical and analytical and take their own skills and strengths and put them to some use. I have a lot of conviction about staying in Iraq. We should not leave, and that's because of the work we did, and I believe in that work. We confronted an enemy that easily would have chosen to bomb a café or kill innocent civilians. [Paul] Bremer [the civilian head of Iraqi's transitional government] disbanded the Iraqi army and police. That was a bad thing to do. You just don't take away security forces. It's the only way a government can protect itself. You can't take that away and then not take on the full security responsibility. We should have gone in with a much bigger troop strength. It was amazingly stupid what we did. Now what we are trying to do is set up a new army and police force, and we haven't done that very well. We ask people to sign up in droves, and then it's so easy for the recruits to be killed. Iraq sucks, and it's a tough tour duty. I think we need to get out, but our mission is to give Iraq back what we took away from it, which is a security force.

It's not a war to win. We are not going to make Baghdad look like Wichita, Kansas, or improve the quality of life for Iraqis. They have to do it themselves. Iraq can't be our 51st state. I believe we should stay there and fight against the people Iraq has no means to fight against. They don't deserve this. We gave the insurgents the opportunity to do this to the Iraqi people. I was more than happy to engage with them. Shoot at me. Don't shoot at these innocent kids or recruits. It would be morally wrong to leave Iraq. We are all they got.

PATRICK MURPHY

Army Captain
Lives: New Hope, Pennsylvania
Iraq War Service: July 2003–January 2004

When I landed at Baghdad Airport, my guys from the 82nd Airborne picked me up in a convoy, handed me a weapon, a couple of magazines, and said, "Load up. We are going through the city. We are driving through ambush alley." I knew then I was going to the Super Bowl of war.

We were a combat brigade of 3,500 people. These are the guys on the front line, the tip of the spear. We were in Al Rashid, the biggest and poorest district. There were 1.5 million people, the size of Philadelphia. My dad was a police officer for 22 years in Philadelphia. There are 1.5 million people in Philadelphia and 7,000 police officers. There are 1.5 million people where we were, and there were 3,500 of us. There were less law enforcement people in that Iraqi city, in the middle of a war, than there are in Philadelphia right now. Then I hear my government say we are not short-handed.

I worked 20-hour days. I was in bed by 1:30 A.M. and up by 6 A.M. Nineteen guys from the brigade died. Every time a guy died, I had to work on the investigation. I was the brigade's attorney, and I had seven paralegals working with me. We practiced every kind of law imaginable—criminal law, international law, foreign claims, and even family law. You'd have guys come into the office, shut the door, and start bawling because their wife of 20 years was leaving them because they were supposed to be home the Fourth of July, and it's now September, and their wife was tired of the pace.

War brings out the best and the worst in you. Unfortunately, we had to court-martial 18 of our men in my time there. I had three guys who took Valium while on guard duty at night and passed out. Their headquarters was a truck factory with a fence around it. Someone could have walked in and killed all of them. So they were court-martialed. We had 110 cases of Article 15s[1] for fistfights and things like that.

Sometimes the troops went into the wrong house and bust down doors, jumped through windows, or got into a car accident. We would admit when we were wrong and set up a claims system. I didn't have enough personnel, so I hired Iraqi attorneys.

I adjudicated 1,600 claims by Iraqis and paid out over $200,000. So if a tank went over a car, I'd give them $2,500 for a new car. It was like that person hit the lottery because $2,500 was 10 years of salary.

I also bought three Iraqis for prosecution in their Iraqi Central Criminal Court, in what was their version of the Supreme Court. One was Sheik Moyad, a very radical Shiite cleric and lieutenant of Muqtada al-Sadr's. He put his nose up at the Americans. There was high unemployment, and he got people fired up threatening to kill Americans. So every Friday when they had their sermons, he said he

---

[1]Nonjudicial punishment by a commanding officer or officer in charge to members of his or her command for minor disciplinary offenses.

would bring death to Americans. He kept mortar, grenades, AK-47s, all kinds of weapons in his mosque, which was completely against the Geneva Convention and international law. He kidnapped three Iraqis, stole generators, threatened to kill my brigade commander and battalion commanders, and did things he shouldn't be doing. That was the best court case I ever tried. I worked my tail off to learn the 1969 Iraqi Criminal Code. He went to jail for seven years.

When he was first arrested, 1,000 people protested. We had to shut down Highway 8, which was like I-95, a six-lane highway. The people who protested weren't even from our district, but they were Muqtada al-Sadr's men bused up from the south, waving flags and blocking off the road. They wouldn't let ambulances go by, and they said, "No, it's Allah's will if they die." This is a decision we had to make. Do we let them protest on the road? We'd just supplemented Iraqi law, giving them freedom of speech, but like America, it's not an absolute right. You can't stand in the middle of I-95 and hold a billboard. We said, "You can protest, but you need to ask for a permit." So we told the people, "You need to get off the roadway." We had tanks come in and blocked them and pushed them off. While the guys were doing that, someone threw a grenade and seriously injured eight of our paratroopers. No one knew where it came from, but no shots were fired from us. If that's not a testament to the will power of the American soldier, I don't know what is. Eventually we pushed them back, and no protestors were hurt.

☆　☆　☆

I trained 600 Iraqi soldiers in small class settings. I taught rules of engagement, but I also taught them what it meant to be a soldier. I'd tell them about the seven army values: loyalty, duty, respect, selfless services, honor, integrity, and personal courage. I told them to be loyal to their country. I spent a lot of time with them. I told them, "You are my brothers now. We are brothers in arms. In history we fought like the dickens with the Japanese and the Germans and look now. Ten years from now, I'm going to come to Iraq on vacation and visit my brothers. We are brothers now in the same profession, with the same goal: a better Iraq. This is a defining moment in your country's history, and you are true patriots for your country."

I took the job very seriously. I could have sent my guys to train them, and they did help, but I wanted to do it. I could have stayed behind the desk, but that's not leadership, sitting behind the desk. You have to go out there and touch and feel things. It was a big deal to have a captain teach a class. They knew the rank of captain. I didn't talk down to them. It was a 45-minute class, and then we'd break into small groups. I went around and had them tell me their names and about their families. I told them about my fiancée and my family. We didn't have uniforms for them, and a uniform is important for a soldier. We had a bunch of Chicago White Sox caps, and we created a makeshift uniform for them. We wanted them to have the pride of wearing a uniform.

When I came back from Iraq in January, we had a week of leave. I was engaged to be married to a girl who told me in October she wasn't sure if she could do this anymore. I knew in my heart it was over. So when I came back home, I saw her and asked her what was going on, but I knew in my heart. She said, "I can't do this anymore. I'm not in love with you." That's a tough thing to come home to after war. Luckily my parents were there. They had driven down to my base in North Carolina from Pennsylvania. The next day I showed up at my parents' hotel and I told them. I broke down like a baby and cried.

I received the Bronze Star[2] for my service in Iraq. I didn't get the Bronze Star for one defining moment. I wasn't like Rambo with my shirt off, saving lives. It was for my work overall. I was honored to get it. I did little things, you know. By the end of the day at 1 A.M., after 20 hours of work, my men were on the roof with the big machine gun watching over us, and I'd go up there and bring them a cup of coffee and say, "How are you doing?" I'd shoot the breeze with them, make sure they were all right. I'm proud my team all came home alive.

---

[2]Awarded to any person who, while serving in the military, distinguishes him- or herself in combat by heroic or meritorious service, not involving aerial flight.

I decided to leave the military. I felt I had given it everything I could for 11 years, 5 years on active duty. I was deployed twice, one time to Bosnia. I also taught constitutional law at West Point. I barely took a vacation. I wanted to settle down, get married, and have kids. It was time to go home.

The greatest thing I'll ever have done in my life was to serve my country in Iraq. I felt like I was changing the world for the better. I'm running for Congress in 2006, and I am going to win, but that won't be as great an accomplishment as serving in Iraq.

The most important issue out there is that we are a nation at war, and you wouldn't know that by walking down the streets of Philadelphia or into a Starbucks right now. But I know it. I saw it. I walked with those troops in Baghdad, and it breaks my heart to see the direction our country is going, and it's time to stand up. It would be easy to sit in this law firm and make all the money I never had. But I think we need more leadership in Washington, people who are going to vote their conscience. I'm not antiwar. I'm not prowar—I'm protroops. I have very liberal people in my party who are upset with me because I am not antiwar. They don't think I'm taking a strong enough stance, but it's hard to be antiwar when you were a part of it. It's hard to say the war wasn't right when I know that will dishonor the people I served with. It's hard to have conservatives question my patriotism. I know what I have done for my country, and I'm not afraid to take a stand. The administration can go up there and say they support the troops. They can take pictures with troops, give speeches in front of the troops, but the fact is they are not supporting the troops. The VIPs who came and visited us—they have up-armored humvees as their vehicles. Why shouldn't a private have that? Why are veterans' benefits being cut and VA hospitals being closed when over a million Iraq War veterans are home? So when veterans have bad dreams and they need help, they have no place to go. That's what we are doing to our veterans out there, and it's a disgrace, an absolute disgrace.

HEROLD NOEL

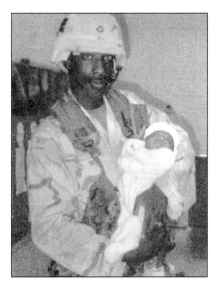

Army Private First Class

Lives: Bronx, New York

Iraq War Service: January 2003–September 2003

I've tried to commit suicide twice. I put a gun to my head and pulled the trigger. I did that when I was living out of my car, when I was homeless. I couldn't provide for my family. It's embarrassing. It's all embarrassing. I expected to come back from Iraq as a hero, not a zero. I don't think anybody cares.

I went to the driver's license place in New York because my license expired while I was in Iraq. The woman there said I had to pay $45. At that time, I was broke. I just came back from Iraq. I was like, "Yo, my sergeant had told me when I got back home, they would renew soldiers' licenses for free." So I showed her my orders, my military ID, and asked for a renewal. The lady said it's not for free. She said nothing is for free. She said, "I don't care that you were in Iraq. You didn't fight for me. You fought for Bush, so I don't really care. Where's the $45?" I started thinking, us soldiers, we are out there killing people, doing things we didn't want to do, and for what? For these ingrates, these motherfuckers who don't give a fuck, drinking their lattes every morning. They don't give a damn that there are people's kids and fathers fighting out there so they can go through their normal day. This is the thanks we get? It makes no sense. I started thinking that everyone was like that. I started walking around with a gun on me and thought the first person who says something to me, I am going to beat the hell out of them. That was how mad I was, and I'm still mad. No one cares. That's why when I came home, I ended up homeless.

When I came back, I really wanted to reenlist, but I had to get out, to breathe, but when I came back to New York, I couldn't find anywhere to stay. Rent in New York—come on, it's ridiculous. I went to Section 8, welfare, the VA, and they all denied me. I had back injuries from an explosion. You think they paid me for anything? Nope, they denied me.

I was living out of my car, a red 1993 Jeep. My furniture was everywhere. We had no place to stay. My wife's mother's house was small, and she had my wife's sister and brother staying there. We tried to stay with my sister-in-law, but she had a small room, and she had kids, so I had to find a place to stay. All my stuff stayed in my car. I had to change in my car, some nights I slept in my car, but I always made sure my family had a place to sleep.

I have twins by another woman. I had to have them move in with their mother. They went back to Florida. I had custody but no place to live. I was not mentally right, and we were living in and out of shelters, and I even had my clothes stolen. I didn't want my kids to see that. I didn't fight for this country to come back and stay at a shelter.

At one point we were staying with these people, but when they left, we had to leave. You know how uncomfortable that is? When they get up to go to work, you got to leave. So I stayed in my car and drove around all day. My wife had a little job. Paying $8 an hour. That wasn't going to get us anywhere, and we had a baby son. It was hard for me, and I was just coming back from Iraq. I couldn't even take care of myself, and I had to come back and fight another freakin' war just to get some help. I never knew how it felt to be homeless. It was a culture shock for me to have nowhere to go. There was no help. When you are discharged, you are on your own.

When I was homeless, I wanted to go back in. There was nothing out here but a bunch of hypocrites arguing about the war. I was watching TV one time, and they had something on about homeless hawks, and all these people were protesting. My daughter is looking me and says, "Daddy, how come they are protesting for homeless hawks and not us?" It broke my heart. People don't care. They don't care about humans. They care more about a dog getting killed on the street or a homeless dog than a homeless man. I told my daughter that is how life is.

People were frightened during 9/11, but that was a wake-up call to these people who drink their lattes and think life is so sweet. It's probably going to happen again. Next time it happens, it may be a soldier who does something, a soldier who just doesn't give a damn. There was a soldier in California who started killing people—he was messed up in the head. I am just waiting for the first disgruntled soldier to walk in that building and blow that shit up. You are mistreating these soldiers and putting them out in the street. What's going to happen when the soldier is an explosive expert? He is going to say, "Fuck this. I am going to make them feel my pain." It'll be like 9/11. Timothy McVeigh, the D.C. sniper—people see them as crazy, but you have to look into their minds to see why they did it. Look at all the Vietnam veterans sleeping on the streets. How long is it going to take before Iraq vets come back and they are sleeping on the streets, too? It's just repeating itself. I know an Iraq vet who is sleeping in a shelter now, but she doesn't want to go to the media. I told her to follow my route, but she didn't want to do it. She said people lying to her and feeding her dreams have messed her up. She can't deal with it anymore. She has been in that shelter two years. She was pregnant and had her baby in that shelter.

* * *

I'm not sleeping; I take naps in the day. The first thing I do in the morning when I get up is take a drink. I never drank before. I used to hate the taste of liquor. Now I drink all the time. I've tried to work, but I am under so much medication for depression and antipsychotic medicine. I'm like a zombie.

Sometimes you feel like giving up. Sometimes I'd be thinking, "What good am I to my kids or my wife?" I can't even sleep good. My kids are just going to grow up to be scared of me. My wife is scared of me. She may leave me. I ain't good for nothing, and that's why I feel like giving up. No one cares. I'll keep saying that's true until I see that people care.

The little apartment I got now, the furniture, my benefits, my back pay—everything I got is because of the media. The media showed me living out of my freaking car. People read my story, two weeks passed, and no one reached out. Not the black community or the Haitian community—my parents are Haitian—no one reached out. Then this anonymous millionaire came forward. I don't know who he is. I just know he is a rich white guy. He offered to pay my rent for a year because the VA denied me everything. Then, when the VA read the story, they finally gave me my benefits.

* * *

Let me tell you why I joined the military. I was a kid from the hood. There was nothing changing around me. I was getting in trouble, and everyone was dying around me or getting locked up. I started having kids when I was young. I was 17 when my twin girls were born. I didn't want to be a deadbeat dad. I wanted to better myself. I didn't want to end up another statistic of a black kid, selling drugs on the street. I joined the military in 2000. I was 19.

We left for Kuwait in January 2003, and I was part of the initial invasions. They told us to take over Baghdad Airport, and then that's it—you go home. I thought the minute we reached Iraq, we would be in Baghdad Airport. I don't know nothing about Iraq. I'm

a young black kid from the hood. I don't know my *National Geographic*. I didn't know none of that stuff. I am just trying to make a living for my family. Our colonel, before we left, gave a big speech. He told us to look to your right and left, that our buddies may not come back. That's when it dawned on us that we could die. You could not imagine your buddy is not going to come back. You can't believe that until you see your first dead body and they're dropping bombs. It's crazy, real crazy. No one will ever understand. It was like a nightmare times 2,000. It's like something you thought you would never get out of.

The hardest thing about being in Iraq is being in Iraq. Those people live in fear every day. They don't know if a bomb is going to drop on their house. They are scared to walk the streets. You can see it in their faces. I felt sorry for them. These people, they believe when they die, they are going to get 18 virgins. They believe that, so how do you take over a land like that? This is a religious war for them. You can't change these people. This a never-ending fight unless you just throw a nuclear bomb and annihilate everybody because these people—the men, women, and even the kids—they will all keep coming at you.

I was in one ambush, and we were in a truck. We were supposed to go turn in some ammo and get some more. We were in Fallujah. The truck in front of us that was holding soldiers blew up—you know what I'm saying: "Boom!" then a pile of smoke. I started coughing. There was black smoke everywhere. It was hot. Your skin was burning. I got out of the truck, and people were firing. A couple of my buddies caught shrapnel in their face. My other boy, he was just there shooting, and I saw that his leg was blown off. He was in the truck in front of us. They had run over a bomb. It was mayhem. You didn't know where to shoot. You're dizzy, hot. It was so crazy.

When you get ambushed, you have these people trying to stop your truck. They stand right in the middle of the road, and they would get the kids to do it, too, and you're left with no choice but to run them over. What can you do? Sit there and die, or run these motherfuckers over? Nobody wanted to do it. People have kids and loved ones to go back home to.

You shoot in the direction that they are shooting at you. You don't know if you kill them. If they drop, they drop. I'm not going to sit here and say how many people I killed. I'm not proud of it. I don't want to take someone's life. Every day I wake up and think someone is going to take my life. I did what I had to do, what I was ordered to do. Sometimes, my back was up against the wall. It was either my life or theirs.

One day we were driving, one of the tanks flipped over in a ditch. So we all had to stop, pull guard duty, and secure the area. The fuelers stayed in the middle, and I'm a fueler. So everything is secure, and daylight hits. There was this sandstorm the night before, and it was pitch black at night, so we had to wait until the sandstorm died down. So when the sun comes up and everything clears, the first thing we see is a crowd of people, who are standing there, waiting. We got paranoid, and we tell them to back up.

Meanwhile, a bigger tank comes and pulls the tank out of the ditch. Suddenly as we are about to pull off, this lady appears out of nowhere and starts walking toward us. She has something wrapped up in her arms, and she is walking real slow toward my truck. I don't know how she got past the soldiers. They are all telling her to stop. I have my M-16, and I'm like saying in Iraqi, whatever, to stop, but she doesn't—she keeps walking. No one knows if she's carrying a bomb or what. So shots were fired, and the lady falls. Whatever was in her hand falls and rolls. Then you see the hand of a baby come up from the wrap, and it's crying. Everyone was like, "Wow." The lady got shot in the head by mistake; it wasn't meant for that. We tried to shoot her in the leg, but soldiers are paranoid. They didn't want to get close to her. I did it. I shot her. It wasn't my fault. I didn't mean for it to hit her in the head. Then the baby was lying there. I was stunned. I was like, "Damn." I don't know what to do. I was frozen. The baby was crying; it was moving its hands. When I took the first step to pick up the baby, another convoy came zooming by and ran over the baby. The baby was all tangled up and started rolling. Its head came off. The body rolled in one direction, the head in another. The baby's body was all tangled up and just rolling, and then truck after truck after truck rolled over it. It was sick, and it haunts me every day. I can't make it stop.

Me being a man seeing children get killed, knowing I have kids. I saw one little girl get her head blown off. You don't think I see my kids' faces when they say fire, and I pull the trigger? Your innocence was lost. It was like you were raped. I always tell people I left my soul back in Iraq.

Sometimes I fall asleep crying. I'm like, "Damn, for what?" I imagine the guys with missing limbs, imagine what they go through inside. They gave up a limb. I gave up my soul. I came back as an amputee, but you can't see my amputation. My amputation is up here, in my head, and no one can give it back to me. I just live every day and wonder if I'm going to die, if the suffering will stop.

Sometimes I just wait for my wife to be sick and tired of being sick and tired. Waiting for her to say she is fed up, tired, and leaving me. Sometimes I think my kids are better off without me. The daddy who went to Iraq stayed in Iraq and died in Iraq. The daddy that came back is a different person.

People are scared of death, but it may be a wonderful thing because you don't have to struggle or suffer anymore. I'm not scared of death—just the way I'm going to die. I don't want to suffer. Sometimes I try to overdose. If you leave here now, there is no guarantee you will see me tomorrow, but I am a survivor. My son is keeping me going. He is two years old, and I think he is the only one who understands me. He is what is keeping me alive.

I'm going to turn 26 soon, and I'm going to sit here and get drunk. I'm scared to go out. I'm scared to take a train. I can't be around too many people. I was never one to complain about this country, but damn, don't you think if you put your life on the line for this country, you deserve something? I hear things in my head all the time, like kids crying, bombs going off, shit like that. I left one war to go to another. I left the physical war, and now I'm in a mental one.

JERMEL DANIELS

Marine Corporal

Lives: New York, New York

Iraq War Service: July 2004–January 2005

I lost my leg because of an IED, a homemade bomb, and it
sucks to be like this.

We were on our way back to the base, which was a power plant
that supplied all the power to Baghdad, in four humvees. I'm a machine gunner, so my job is to be on top of the humvee, manning the
machine gun. The humvees have something on it we call an "ice-
box." It's a jammer, which means it jams up the frequencies of the
bombs so if you go by one, it won't blow up on you. We only had
two. They were on the first and the last vehicles. I was on the second vehicle, which didn't have it. So the first vehicle goes by, nothing happens, and then my vehicle goes by and "Boom"—there's a

big explosion, and it blows up the humvee. It shot me out of the hole, 35 feet in the air. When they found me, I was in the ditch where the bomb blew up. This bomb, it left two big craters on the side of the road, and they were really deep. Everyone jumped out of the vehicle, and someone saw me, and one of my boys pulled me out of the ditch. Our vehicle had completely blown up. The grenades and the ammo in it started shooting off and blowing up.

There were five of us in the vehicle. Three died instantly; two of us survived. The other guy had some bad fractures. He didn't lose any limbs. I lost my leg.

I was up for the whole accident. I couldn't feel anything from the waist down. I was in shock the whole time. My two friends ran over to me and tried to help until the captain came over. He stopped the bleeding, and he tried to calm me down.

Afterward my guys just lit up the neighborhood. They were pissed. They saw a guy running away, and they took care of him.

They transported me to one of the vehicles and rushed me to the base. They injected me with morphine to beat the pain. The next thing I know I'm lying on a table and can't remember anything. They were trying to revive me. I stopped breathing two times. The shock trauma teams were there. They had to slice down my stomach because in Iraq, they had no X-ray machines. They had to make sure my organs were all right. After that, I don't remember anything else. When I woke up, I was at the medical center in Bethesda, Maryland. I had no idea where I was. I had been in a coma for two weeks. When I woke up, my arms were strapped down to the sides of the bed, and I had a long tube that went through my mouth and down into the center of my chest to help me breathe. I could not pull it out.

I found out I lost my leg when I came out of my coma and looked down at my leg. I cried. It was a bad moment for me, very painful. My right leg was in traction, with pins going through it. I had a lot of wounds and had skin grafts all over. My right leg had a huge hole in it; it was blown wide open after the explosion.

They said they tried to save my other leg, but the blood flow wasn't there. It's sad. I really do wish I had my leg. It kills me every day when I wake up and look down and it's like, "Wow, I have one leg."

It's very tough and frustrating. You get depressed being here. I have my prosthetic, but my other leg is injured so bad, I have to wait to walk on it. I've had three surgeries so far where they had to fuse my ankle. I thank God every day I'm alive. How many people can say they've been blown up and are still alive to tell the tale?

My wife is OK, but we went through a point in the relationship that it was looking kind of rocky. It was hard. I'm here in Walter Reed Hospital, and she's in New York. I was losing her. She was slipping through my clutches. She wanted to get a divorce. I got depressed and really sad. I tried really hard to work on stuff. It took a while, but we worked on it, and now everything is better, thank God. It feels great when I am with her. We have been married for two years but have been together for seven. It's hard for her. She is doing everything herself. She's working and taking care of my son. I love her to death. I don't know any other woman who would do this.

My son misses me like crazy. He is five years old. I want to run and play with him, but, you know, now I can't do much. In the beginning, when I was in the hospital, he was scared. He wouldn't come near me, but now he is used to the way I look. I want to be around him, but what can I do?

They rarely come down here. Last time was two months ago, but I talk to them every day. I usually go to New York to see them as much as I can on the weekends. My apartment in New York isn't wheelchair accessible, so I have to stay in a hotel.

$*$ $*$ $*$

I joined the marines because I wanted to get out of my neighborhood, the projects on the Lower East Side. I wanted to do right by my family. The neighborhood was falling apart. A lot of the kids I grew up with are out there hustling drugs. I didn't want my son doing the same thing. Now I get mad because I want to be home with my wife and my kid, and I can't do it. I can't even get in my

apartment. It's kind of embarrassing, you know. I go to the lobby—there's two elevators, but I have to have my wheelchair lifted up the three steps into the building, and my wife can't do it. She's not that strong. So one of the guys comes down and helps me up the stairs. Then I get into the elevator, and when I get to the door, it's so narrow, and as soon as you get in, you have to go through a narrow hallway. In order for me to get into the bedroom, it's kind of embarrassing. I have to get on the floor and crawl to the bed. I don't like my son to see me like that. My son has a skateboard, and one time, I tried that. I put my body on the board and dragged my arms across the floor to the bedroom. It's embarrassing that I have to go through that, you know. I want to spend time with them. For me to spend the night, for me to go to the bathroom, I can't get up. So when I go to New York, I stay in the Doubletree Hotel.

I get pissed off every day. I want to go for a run. I want to go for a walk. I want to stand up and go to the bathroom. Everything I do is sitting. I'm tired of sitting. I was a very active person. This sucks.

Most of the guys here are 18, 19, and 20. I'm 26, and I'm the old guy here. Most of us are missing limbs. It hurts them every day, like it hurts me. When I get out of here, it will be rough. I'm going to have a prosthetic leg. My ankle is fused so my only leg will have no bend it in for the rest of my life. But you can't dwell on it. I used to be very angry. But you just can't sit there feeling sorry for yourself. You have guys here who are worse them me, missing two legs, two arms, and an eye. I have been here at Walter Reed for a long time. The accident happened eight months ago, and I have a long way to go. I don't know when I'll get out of here. I have a lot of rehab ahead of me. But I am trying to stay positive. I know things will get better. I'm trying not to dwell on the negative.

Sometimes when I'm asleep, I dream I see myself walking, running, and everything is all right again. I'm so happy. Then I wake up, and I'm back to the reality of this.

JAQUAIE MCATEE

Marine Sergeant

Lives: Pittsburgh, Pennsylvania

Iraq War Service: January 2003–September 2003 and
January 2004–May 2004

I work at Sunrise Senior Citizens, an assisted living place,
just basically working with the elderly. I help them get
dressed in the morning, take them to dinner, and help
them eat. On football game days, I work in security for the Pittsburgh Steelers. But I've done two tours in Iraq and one in Afghanistan.
I was a combat engineer, a sergeant, a squad leader, and I handled
mines, bombs, and explosives.

I never thought I would have to use my skills, but as soon as
September 11 happened, we went straight to Afghanistan, and that's
all we did was deal with land mines. They said there were at least

two land mines for every person that was out there. We left December 1, as soon as they found out who did it. I spent Christmas 2001 in the Middle East, sitting on a ship, getting ready to go to Afghanistan. It was cold, freezing cold.

We flew in helicopters all the time, checking out spots, clearing out land mines. We had a couple of altercations, but it wasn't very serious. There were others there that went first.

In the marines, we don't defuse land mines. We'd take a block of C4,[1] put it about six inches away from the mine, and blow it up in place. Anything can be booby-trapped. So you go in thinking even if it's a U.S. mine, you didn't put it there, and there could be a grenade underneath it. I was there for six months. Soon as we came back I was hearing about Iraq. They were like, "Stand back for Iraq." I was like, "What? What is going on in Iraq?"

I went to Kuwait in January 2003. We were on the front, front line. We were the ones that cleared the land mines so that the trucks and tanks could get through. We took down the fences at the border. We were under attack the whole time. I was shooting, running, trying to scream commands out, talking to my boys. There was so much stuff going on. We'd go clear a lane out and basically mark it so the drivers knew where to go. I was a 21-year-old sergeant in charge of marines who are like 27, and I'm dealing with explosives. I was barely old enough to drink, and I was commanding troops. I had their lives in my hands. That first time in Iraq, we found over 2,000 land mines. One day, we found half of them just in a vat in the middle of the road on a strip of land with some trees around it. These people came up to us and said that the bad guys dropped some stuff. We get up there, see there are crates upon crates of these land mines, over 1,000 mines. It's like someone backed up a crate of mines and just dumped them there. There were little kids picking them up.

We got to a couple of scenes too late. The man who taught me everything I know about land mines and explosives stepped on a land mine in Iraq. He was the most proficient marine I ever met. He

[1]A high-quality, very high-velocity plastic explosive.

made me into the marine I am now. He stepped on a land mine and blew his leg off. It was ironic; he had a tattoo of a red triangle mine sign on his right leg. That is the same leg he stepped on the land mine with. What are the chances of that? The man that teaches you everything about land mines steps on one himself. That teaches you that you are vulnerable.

My first firefight in Iraq was right across the Kuwait and Iraq border. We got ambushed. We were passing out MREs [meals ready-to-eat] because these people were starving. We had been bombing them for a couple of hours. That night we were ambushed by the same guys we were feeding all day long. They were young men, like me. We never thought they were bad guys. We are pulling out, and all you hear is "ping, ping, ping" off of the side of our vehicles. All you could see was tracers coming at our vehicles. People are shooting in your direction, and you have to get out and do something. You can't even think about it. We didn't lose anyone that night. We came out on top and punched up north. I, unfortunately, killed people in Iraq. You are going to have to squeeze a trigger here and there. I was pretty accurate with my M-16. That became my baby real quick.

We saw fighting holes, trenches, and uniforms. They—the insurgents—didn't wear uniforms, just regular clothes, so you didn't know who was the enemy. We found trenches with the same MREs we were giving the people in them. They would take the food from us and go to their trenches and wait to kill us. We were supposed to pass out humanitarian rations, but I wondered each time who these people were. We gave a ration to this little kid, and this man just grabbed him and slammed his neck and shoulders for the food. I just wanted to let loose. That disgusted me to see a grown man, like 30, slam a 12-year-old kid right on his neck and shoulders for one bag of food. At first the kid tried to fight him for it. But the man just grabbed him and, wham, slammed him real hard. There was nothing we could do. We were moving and just throwing the rations out of the vehicles. There was nothing you could do.

One time, we saw a tank blown up in the middle of the road. It was like, damn, whatever it was, we don't want it to hit us. Later on, we found out it was a suicide bomber. He came up and pulled up next to them in car, and blew himself up and blew off the right side of the tank. The crew wasn't even hurt. The crew then blew the tank up. That suicide bomber got his rocks off on that tank but didn't even hurt anybody. They believe if they die for a cause, they are going to heaven. They go crazy over there.

We saw kids picking up mines all the time. Some of the land mines looked like toys. They came in different colors. We called them "toe poppers." They have wings on them, and little kids pick them up and throw them like toys. We use a lot of explosives and mines over there, and not all of them go off. I've seen big U.S. bombs that didn't detonate. We went through minefields where some were not even armed, but it still stops you for the same amount of time. Whether it's armed or not, we'd blow it up anyway. It works for the insurgents because it slows us up. They put land mines in the middle of the street, on a regular city or town street, because they know if we're coming to a minefield, we are not just going to keep going. We are going to stop and figure it out.

We left after they declared the war was over. I thought that was the end of everything. I was like, "I made it back from Iraq. I made it back from Afghanistan." I got like six months. I'm chilling, going to do my little bit of time, and then I am getting out and going to college. I was down to four months left, and the war was over, but then it turns out the army was getting hit pretty bad. When they declared the war was over, they took most of all the marines out. We are way smaller than the army, but we move faster. Once we left, the insurgents kept banging them, and they sent us right back. I had 114 days left, and they said if you got 118 days or more left, you are going back to Iraq. I was like, "Hmm, I don't have 118, and I'm going to college." They said I had to go anyway. I had been to war twice for our country. Was someone trying to kill me? Is someone trying to take me out? What is this? What is going on? I ran up the chain of command. It didn't work, and I was sent to war for the third time.

The first time we went in, we had people who liked us, who were like, "Hello, America. Hello. How are you? Hello, mister." We were talking to people, learned a little bit of the language. But the second time it was way worse. This time, we are getting mean stares. You look into crowds, and the guys would look at you and turn away, or stare at you real hard and mean, like they wanted to do something to you, but they can't because you are with all your crew. They look at you like you personally did something wrong to them, which was crazy. The second time I went back, I was in Fallujah, one of the worst combat areas in Iraq. It was during the major offensive, the first since the war was declared over.

Fallujah used to be the base for Saddam's generals, and outside of that base is Fallujah town. We went into that town and cleared out the insurgents. They had tunnels underneath the houses linking house to house. We believed in overwhelming force superiority, which means we are going to shoot the hell out of whoever shoots at us, with everything we got, so they know what we are all about.

So we had these people pop out of houses way down the street, and so we attack them. Then "Bam!" Down the street we are getting attacked again, and the house we were shooting at first stopped shooting. It's like, what happened? They were playing games with us, but we didn't know there were tunnels under the ground. We'd go in the house and find out these guys were going through linking tunnels. So we would blow up a whole house, and there would be no one in there. They'd go to another house. We even got shot at from the mosques, and we can't go in mosques because they are holy ground.

In Fallujah, it was so crazy. In Iraq, every man is allowed to have an AK-47. So basically, you have to think everyone in Iraq has an AK. In every house, you have to be prepared to face machine-gun fire. One time, we went into a house. The man was like, "Yes, America, come in." Then he steps back and says, "I love America." We are like, "OK, cool." Next thing you know, someone is standing behind him with an AK-47, and he opens up. First marine in got hit right in the neck and died. That was the wake-up. We are not playing with these cats. That guy set us up. He knew his guy was in there, and he knew that dude was going to do something, and he just let us get sprayed by this clown. Needless to say, the

threat was eliminated, and the guy who opened up the door was taken care of, too.

There was one house where this guy would not stop shooting. This guy was barricaded in his house, and I didn't even know what kind of weapon he had. I never heard of a weapon like this before, but it was something serious. It was like a machine gun, a heavy machine gun. This guy, he shot one marine, and we knew he was in that house. This was one of the houses with the tunnels in them. So we had the tanks come. We shot the whole house up with thousands of rounds. M-16, all kinds of things. We Swiss-cheesed this house. We threw tear gas, blew it up, we set it on fire and collapsed the roof, and we were still taking shots from this corner house. We were like, "What the hell is going on? Where is he at?" We couldn't figure out how he was still alive. The whole roof imploded, and this guy was still shooting. He would shoot and run. When we pounded, he'd run over to the next house. We even had tanks come. The street was so small it was basically like the tank was putting its muzzle right to the front door. It went straight through the house. We leveled this house, and then we set it on fire. We let it burn, and we were still getting shot at from this house. We called for air to drop bombs on it. We knew he was there, and he shot one of our people. We didn't want to let him go. We found out down the line that these cats were on drugs.

We had this one guy, he came up in a van. We fired a warning shot to let them know to turn around, and if you don't stop, we'll fire anther one. We really didn't want to kill nobody. You'd rather they stop and know what we are talking about than kill them. But these guys were blatantly disregarding our warnings, so we opened up on them. One guy, who is hit, stumbled out of the van, with a dazed look, and walks to the back of the van and grabs an AK and starts spraying and shooting in our direction. We are like, "Damn, this guy is like Superman." We had a sniper who put him down, and now he is on the ground, and he is reaching for the AK. If he can reach it, he is going to kill somebody. I'm like, "What the hell? This guy should be dead." He was hit a whole lot of times with some big guns. We found out that these guys were on something like speed. They would take the drugs before they would get into a firefight so they could be hit a few times and keep going because of the adrenaline. It was crazy, because it was a whole other element to it. If you shot first, you were usually all right, but sometimes you couldn't shoot first. These guys were all doped up. They were like zombies. We were finding syringes and stuff. It all started coming together. That's why they are not lying down when we hit them. They are drugged up. It's just like angel dust. I remember once I saw on *COPS*, the TV show, a guy was being chased by the police. He jumped off a building, broke both his legs, and kept running, and that's what it looked like to me. They were mutilated and still moving around. It was ridiculous.

Fallujah was the wildest place I've ever been in my life, seriously. When I left, we were still in Fallujah. We had 12 men in my squad. I was happy. I wanted to get out of there. In Fallujah, we were getting pounded every day by mortars. It was unnerving. People firing the mortars were the ones who worked on that base before we took over. They knew how to do it right. I was excited to leave, but I didn't want to leave my boys.

Everyone who goes to Iraq gets a psych evaluation. I got nothing. I got a little medical checkup and was out. I'm fine. I'm not having any problems. I'm blessed. I've been through a lot of wild stuff. Not every day you walk through a minefield and come back. I'm not crazy. I'm not having any dreams at all about the war. I have no problems.

I went from making $30,00 to $40,000 a year to $7 an hour in a regular job. Once you get out of the military, it's like, "See ya later." I go to school full-time. I'll be done in January with a degree in criminal justice, and I work two part-time jobs. The hardest part is trying to adjust to the loss of income, loss of wages, to struggling. I put my life on the line a few times for the country, and when I got out, it was like, that's it. There is not too much work you can do in the civilian world that utilizes my background. I don't know. It just seems like there is nothing out there for me.

I've gotten no support here. I don't think people here know who I am. I've heard people say that I should be a millionaire or never have to work. One nice lady at the cafeteria at my job always wants to give me my lunch for free because of my service to our country. There's football and baseball players who make millions of dollars to play, but we are out there protecting these cats, and we make $35,000 with benefits included. We are walking through minefields and getting shot at every which way you can think of, and bombs are blowing up all around us. You would think the harder you work, the more you should get paid. But that's not the case.

I didn't support the war or the reason behind it. What are we there for? Our biggest objectives in the beginning of the war was protecting an oil refinery. That seemed kind of crazy, that our first objective would be the oilfields. I'm not a big Bush supporter. I feel he uses us as bullies. That's why I got out. I knew I would have to go back to Iraq if I stayed. Combat engineers, we are in high demand there to look for mines and roadside bombs. Why should I put my life on the line when I didn't even know why? We went into Iraq right after 9/11, and they didn't even have anything to do with it. We haven't even caught the guy who was responsible for 9/11. This war is like a whole other Vietnam.

I am 22 years old, and I have been to war three times. Can you imagine that? I'm a young guy, not an old man, and look at all I've been through.

JULIUS TULLEY

National Guard Sergeant

Lives: Navajo Reservation, St. Michaels, Arizona

Iraq War Service: February 2002–May 2003

I am a 42-year-old Native American. Americans call us Navajo, but we are Diné people. That is what we call ourselves. I am patriotic for my people. I love my people. I served in the army for 17 years: 13 years' active duty and the last 4 in the National Guard. I fought in Iraq for my people, but in some ways, it has killed me. In some ways, I am not the same person I used to be.

My father died two weeks after I came back from Iraq. I think he was waiting for me, and I have not cried for him. We were very close, and I have not shed a tear. My nephew died, and I have not cried for him. I have not laughed since I've been back. All my family and friends would tell you that I have changed. They say, "You used to be so spiritual and humble, so patient, and these are the positive things we miss about you." They say now it's hard to be around me because I'm short-tempered and my spirituality is not as strong. It's been hard for me. It's hard for me to explain, to find the words. I'm just thankful I haven't turned to alcohol.

I wanted to serve. That's what I wanted to do in the midst of war, live as righteously as I could and serve mankind in a good way. But then when I came home, I felt like I did my part in war. I kept myself from doing wrong, and I felt the people of Iraq needed to be released, freed from Saddam the dictator, and I did so. I do feel a connection to the Iraqi people. I respect them. I did my part, came home, and then I tried asking for help, for assistance. I said I needed some psychological help, but my Navajo people, my government, could not help me. They kept saying I needed to go to the outside for that. They said, "We don't have the resources here." They always go back to the same thing—lack of money. Yet so many of us here are veterans.[1] I would think there should be attention paid to my request. I want the same resources and assistance given to Iraq vets everywhere, but we don't have a veterans' hospital on the Navajo reservations. So many Native Americans serve. But when we need help, we have to drive three hours to Albuquerque or five hours to Phoenix or eight hours to Salt Lake City. I don't want a handout. I just want help. We don't have the technology the outside world has. We don't have the Internet in our homes. We don't have much here, and help doesn't filter down to our level, so it is very hard for me right now, very hard to get help.

When I came home, things did not seem real to me. They did in Iraq. I could touch things. I could feel. When I came home, the only thing I felt was real was when I went into my house with my wife and children. There, I could feel the love from them that was real to

----

[1]According to the Department of Defense, Native Americans represent less than 1 percent of the U.S. population yet make up about 1.6 percent of the military. More Native Americans serve in the military per capita than any other minority group.

me, and I felt OK at my mom's house. No one there asked me about Iraq or called me a hero. I am no hero. The heroes are the ones that actually saved lives. Once I stepped out the door, nothing was real anymore.

*   *   *

Sometimes I dream about Iraq. Last week I was at my mom's house, and I went into a room, threw a mattress on the ground, and slept there on the floor, and started dreaming that I was back in Baghdad fighting, killing insurgents. Then I woke up. The room I was sleeping in was empty with just a mattress, so I really thought I was back in Iraq. I felt the walls with my hands, and then I started crawling around the room. But then I came to a door and was like, "Hmm, what is a door doing here?" They don't have doors where I slept in Iraq, and then I felt the doorknob, and I'm like, "Where am I at? Where am I at?" Then I saw the furniture, and I realized I'm back at home and must have had a bad dream. So I'm like, "OK, I'm back home." So I went back to sleep, and immediately I started dreaming again. I'm in the same place this time, but I don't have a weapon, and I ask my NCO [noncommissioned officer], I say, "I need a weapon. I don't have a weapon. I just came from leave, and I was never reissued my weapon. Where's my weapon?" And he says it's across the road, and I can't go out because we are in battle now, and I panic. I say to myself, "I must be dreaming, I must be dreaming." And I force myself to wake up. I was pretty shook up. I need someone to talk to about these things, but my people can't help me.

*   *   *

When I was a little boy, I was taken out of the hogan[2] I shared with my family and put in a boarding school by the American government. It was required that we go to school. Sometimes I

---

[2]A traditional Navajo one-room, round house.

109

only saw my family a couple of times a year. They taught me how to speak English, and after high school, I went to college at Brigham Young University. I did two years there, and I ran out of funding, and the sensible thing to do was to figure out a way to keep going to school and get financial support. So I went into the military even though I didn't really like the idea of it. I was a newlywed. I was about 23. It was the best option at the time because the GI Bill could pay for school, and any kids we had would be born in a hospital with good medical care.

My three brothers talked bad of war. They said it was ugly, and they told me what they went through in Vietnam. My father served in World War II. But I went in anyway. I didn't feel I had a choice.

I was stationed at Fort Carson, Colorado, which looks just like home, and I came home every other month. When my enlistment ended right before I got my release papers, the commander called me in and said, "Sgt. Tulley, you've done well in the military," and told me if I reenlisted, I was going to Hawaii. I came home, talked to my wife, who said OK. So I reenlisted and kept going on. I wanted to see the world. I went to Fiji, Australia, all the Hawaiian Islands. After that, it kept getting better and better. My wife liked it. By the time we got back home, I was stationed in Kentucky. All my children were born there.

I left the army because of the leadership, and I was missing home—my people, my land, and how I grew up. I didn't want to abandon my people, and I wanted to start assisting my people. The leadership we had in Washington—Clinton—he was shrinking the military, and there were lots of changes, and I didn't like them. They were downsizing the military, and I didn't agree with it. Five months before I was supposed to leave was 9/11. I knew right then that I would be going to war. I wasn't afraid.

I was on active duty, and I was getting out, but it took an extra four months because of what was going on in Iraq. Everyone was on freeze—no leave and no leaving the military. I finally made it home, then joined the guard. I wanted to retire from the military so I could get benefits. I joined the National Guard in Blanding, Utah.

Half of the people there were Navajo. I have a Navajo flag on my helmet along with the American flag, and I keep a picture of my family inside my helmet.

I was with the guard for six months, and then the call came November 2002 to pack everything and come to Blanding. We were told we would have a chance to say good-bye to our families, but I never came home. I was never scared or afraid to go to war and left it all up to a higher power. The hardest part was leaving my family. I have five children.

We trained at Fort Hood, Texas. As I was going through the museum there, I saw pictures of the Navajo people being rounded up, and then I thought this is the very unit, the very divisions, that came over and rounded up my people like animals. This is the very people, the very military, that came over and killed my people. When they killed my people, a lot of our beliefs and traditions were lost. That is something I am struggling with to this day. The only thing is that I'm hoping that what my people went through will never happen again, and I'm not just talking about my Diné, Navajo people. I'm talking about all people, including Iraqis.

They sent us to Fort Lewis in Washington, then to Kuwait. I didn't get to see my parents. We never got to go back, but my wife and kids and brother saw me off.

My family met me two days before I was going to leave for training in Iraq. My mom was concerned because the Navajo ceremony of protection that needed to be done before you go to war didn't happen because we couldn't go home. So we called for a medicine man, and he did the ceremony for us. It's a sacred ceremony. Then I said good-bye to my family.

When I got to Kuwait, we were two weeks into the war. I remember going over there, and it looked so different. There were no deer, no mountains, all desert. It was about 120 degrees. It took some time to get used to it. I went though some more training, and after the training, we headed over to Baghdad. The second night we were hit, but our vehicle only sustained minor damage. That was our first miracle. No one was hurt. We were in a convoy, and we were headed to Baghdad.

Once we got to Baghdad, it was unbelievable to see all the destruction we caused. But I guess these people were used to war. They had been at it for centuries. When we rolled into Baghdad, they were cheering for us. They were happy, and they were clapping. It made us feel good, but we were nervous because we were told to watch out for kids, that they might have explosives. We went through the town and got to the airport, which was our mission spot—Baghdad Airport. Our mission was to clear it. I am a combat engineer. I go in and clear explosive devices that obstruct the troops' movements. The first week we slept in our vehicles until we cleared the mess. The airport was bombed out.

We were attacked 85 percent of the time. I left it all up to the Creator as to what would happen. I was not afraid at all because I depended on the ceremony that was done for me, and I knew that not only my family and friends but people back home and all over the world were praying for us and our safety. I relied on their prayers a lot. I had faith. I was afraid, but not as afraid as some of the other soldiers. I remember my brother was always telling me not to feel alone. There will always be a spiritual being there.

There was no place to hide. We were in the desert. Whenever you go, you are fighting your way through. Everywhere we went, we had a lot of close calls, but we did not lose anyone. I saw a lot of Iraqis get killed. I would try not to look at their bodies. I did not want to see them.

There were all these attacks all the time, and my life was miraculously being spared. Some people would say, "Oh, my, you are lucky," but to me, it was never luck. I was blessed. I fired at a lot of Iraqis. I don't know if I killed any of them. I took no pride in killing another human being. But I would do the killing not to be killed.

It is very hard for me to talk about what I saw, what happened there. I'm trying to get help. I really am. I support the president and what he is doing. I believe in the cause and am proud that I served. I would go back if they asked me. I am a warrior, and my people are warriors. I don't want to go back, but I will.

ALEX PRESSMAN

To Cpl Alex Pressman, USMCR
With best wishes

Marine Reserves Sergeant
Lives: Brooklyn, New York
Iraq War Service: February 2003–July 2003

You can't turn the wheel of life back. You can't live the rest of your life feeling sorry for yourself and asking, "Why did it happen to me?" You have to forget about it and get on with your life and make the best of it.

When I got wounded in Iraq, I was on the back of a convoy doing security. I had volunteered to go to Baghdad to get some medical supplies. I was in the back of the convoy with a machine gun, and the convoy commander told us to stop for a smoke break. We all stopped by a pit off the highway. I had a few guys in front of me talking, waiting on line to take a leak. I wanted to smoke. My buddy was right next to me . . . , and I just stepped on a land mine. It threw me up a little, and then I fell down. Everyone took cover. They thought we were under fire because there was a loud boom. My foot had blown off. There was nothing they could do but give me morphine. It hurt, but they did a tourniquet and stopped the bleeding a little bit. I waited over an hour for a chopper to come and pick me up. It hurt, but I wasn't screaming. I was still a man, but it was very painful. I was like, "Shit, why?" It was not a pleasant thing to look at. My bone was sticking out from where my foot was.

They flew me to Baghdad, and I had my initial surgery that took care of the bone that was sticking out. They cut it out. There was also a chunk of muscle missing from my other leg and multiple lacerations. The next day, I was flown to Germany and spent 10 days there, then to the Bethesda Naval Hospital, where I spent two months. Then they sent me to Walter Reed for a prosthetic and to go through therapy. I was depressed for a while but always had friends and family with me. I kept thinking, "What am I going to do now?" I thought I wouldn't be able to find a job. I thought, "Why did it happen to me?" You know, stupid stuff like that. I was on drugs all the time. It was painful to learn to walk with it. For a year, I just didn't know what to do. I had my moments of depression that was hard to get away from, but I'd snap out of it. Now I'm trying to go on with my life.

President Bush came to see me it when I was at Walter Reed, and it made me feel great. He came in my room. Everyone had to wear gloves in my room because of germs, but he didn't want to. He shook my hand and said, "Thank you for the job you did." He asked where I was from and was surprised that I was an immigrant. He said, "We take care of our veterans." I read they are trying to close Walter Reed Hospital. I don't know what to think. It's huge. All the army guys go to Walter Reed and all of us who lose limbs. I'm against that. You got to find another way. Why don't they close another hospital? Walter Reed is the busiest hospital in the military.

But I support the president, and I support the war. It upsets me when people say bad things about it, especially when people who are saying it have nothing to do with the military. Everyone is entitled to their own opinion, but we, the people who are fighting the war, are not there with our opinions. Whether we are against or for the war, we have to follow orders no matter what. We have to do what the higher-ups tell us to do. We have to finish what we started. It's going to take years. It's not going to be fast.

I'm Russian, and I have something similar to compare it to. Russia was in war with Afghanistan for 10 years. It's the same people and the same mentality. It's a hard war, and it's a hard war to win. When people don't care about their own personal lives, they will use any tactics to hurt the enemy. The only way they fight is roadside bombs and RPG [rocket-propelled grenade] attacks—not a lot you can do about that. It's hard, and there are a lot of casualties. But we are such a big country, so powerful. We need to help out nations who can't help themselves, and what was going on with Saddam's regime—you know, it was really bad. We saw mass graves and people looking for relatives in the mass graves.

People say there were no weapons of mass destruction. We were telling Saddam for three months we were going to attack. If they wanted to, they could have gotten them all out of there. Not finding the weapons yet doesn't mean to me they didn't have them. I want to think that because of the price we paid for it. The sacrifice of the guys—people have to live with it for the rest of their lives. A lot of the stuff you will never forget. We paid a big price for the mission. We started it, and hopefully it was all worth it. It would be a waste of time, waste of lives, if they pulled out. Besides, the guys and girls who are getting killed—there are thousands who are wounded, disabled, not only physically but mentally disabled, too. Some may not even know it now, but it will come up in the future. We just can't pull out now. The whole world is watching us. We would be telling the whole world we made asses of ourselves.

* * *

I am a Russian Jew. I came here when I was 16, to Brooklyn, to Sheepshead Bay. After one semester in college, I decided to join the marines. I always wanted to go into the military. It was a dream I always had. I even liked the military when I was living in Russia. One day there was a recruiter on campus, and I signed up. A month later, I was in training. That was in 1996. I joined the reserves, came

back home, went to college, and started working. I owned a clothing store and also worked managing a medical office. My contract was supposed to expire, and then I got a call that my unit was being activated. I wanted to go and do something. That's what being in the military is about—doing a job to earn the paycheck. We got shipped out December 25, and my contract expired the 30th, but I really wanted to stay. I wanted to go to war. I wanted to be one of the ones who make a difference. I didn't spend six years in the military just to come to work on the base. I wanted to do the real thing. I wanted to experience it, and I don't regret it even though I became disabled because of it.

* * *

After I got out of Walter Reed, I went back to school. The VA is paying for my education, and I am majoring in finance. I want to work for the government. I also got involved with a business with my friend for people who have sleep problems, which are a big problem with veterans. I also have helped to organize Russian-American Servicemen of the Armed Forces, a group that lobbies for veterans' benefits and health care. We got a lot of guys, and we are trying to get it going.

I'm fine, and I'm just trying to get on with my life. I'm not happy I have to walk with a prosthetic, and I get depressed. Sometimes it comes in a wave. I wish it didn't happen, but it did. I can't change it. I have to live my life.

ARIC ARNOLD

Army Major
Lives: Fayetteville, North Carolina
Iraq War Service: August 2003–May 2004

I love America, but don't get me wrong—if I hit that Powerball jackpot for $340 million, I'm gone. I'm not a Pat Tillman[1] type. I love the army because it gave me an opportunity that no other institution would have given me when I was being a knucklehead and flunking out of college. I had a GPA of 1.1 in community college. My car was being repossessed. My car payment was $200 a month. When the repo man came, I had to stop him because the car payment checks were in the glove compartment. I was not very focused.

---

[1]Tillman was a professional football player who gave up a multimillion-dollar contract to join the army. He was later killed in Afghanistan.

My father was a big-time military man in the navy and air force, and I knew I would be in the military. I wanted to be a pilot, but my eyesight wasn't good enough, but I managed to squeak into the army.

I am technically qualified and technically listed as an army aviator. I can fly Chinook helicopters, but for the last three years, I haven't done any aviation flying duties, which is pretty much the case of most army aviators on the commission side. We wind up being in positions outside the cockpit. All the places I wanted to go, the army has allowed me to. Everything I have wanted to do, I've been able to. Don't get me wrong—there have been days when I want to hit someone upside the head, but there really has been very little negatives. I've been able to buy a house we designed from the ground up. Civilians have to put down 10 to 15 percent; we only had to put down $1,200. There was no way I could have afforded it if I weren't in the army. I have had a helluva life and a helluva lot of opportunity. I'm proud of the stuff I've done. All together, I've been in the army for about 14 years.

I was a captain when I was deployed to Iraq. It was a funny situation. Normally a captain commands one unit for 18 months. Fortunately, I had the chance to command three different companies in three years, and the one I went to Iraq with was the third one. The previous company commander was injured in the summer of '03. No one was available to take command over the company I was coming out of, and the situation was placed upon me. I agreed to take the company, and soon after that we were told we were going to be deployed to Iraq.

It was very hectic with long days. I had a great company that I was coming out of and taking over one that was in its third deployment in three years. A lot of people knew what to do, so we went about it, and I don't recall a lot of worry. I really didn't have much time. I'm married with two daughters, 14 and 5, so you are trying to prepare them for your absence. I made sure my wife had knowledge of everything. My wife takes care of the inside, and I did the outside. I needed to find a lawn mower guy. For 90 percent of the soldiers, you don't have time to concentrate on the negatives because you are so busy doing what you need to do. I give all the credit to my wife and daughters. They were very strong. When I told my wife, she was OK. My older daughter was extremely mature about it. My youngest was at an age—I mean, how do you explain on a level she would understand? I had been separated from her for short times, but never in a capacity that I couldn't call every night. But this was war. I didn't know when I would talk to her. I was trying to explain to her what it was all about, that Daddy didn't know when he was coming back. But even at five, she seemed to understand it. She said, "OK, Daddy, but you will come back?" And I said I would.

Because I was so busy, so much got pushed off that was upsetting to the family. We kept putting off a day or a weekend for family stuff, and then it never materialized. Even the day I was due to deploy, I thought they would let me go to work, get a few things done, and then I'd be free to hang out until I had to go on the plane. Unfortunately, I had a boss who was difficult to work with. He did everything he could do take up every bit of that time. I literally just had time to run from my office, kiss my wife and daughters, take a picture with them, and then get on the plane. That was the extent of my family time.

I thought about that picture with my family. If something happened to me, that two minutes I had would be the last thought they would have of me. My youngest wasn't happy, but no one cried. They were very strong. I commend them. I have the deepest respect for them.

I was a company commander for an air traffic control unit. We controlled air space that went over Baghdad. At the time we were there it was the most hostile air environment in Iraq. Nine aircraft were shot down, six in our area of operations. We had the one with the Chinook that lost the 24 lives—the first female aviator killed in combat; the medic aircraft where 11 lives where lost. That was all within our environment and numerous others.

When we first crossed into Iraq, I had a stern conversation with one of my soldiers. Most of them were young, 18 to 24. We were stopped on the side of the road while one of the vehicles was being worked on. These Iraqi kids were impoverished. They had dirty faces and wore dirty clothes. This one soldier, he came from Virginia, and he grew up on the streets. So he sees a kid who looked like that on the side of the road, and he goes and gives the kid some candy. He is trying to do something nice. Well, that one kid turned into 15. Then the soldier was trying to give candy to all these kids so they don't think America is bad. But you don't know who has a bomb, and so I had to go over with an M-16 and shoo those kids away. Then I had to have a conversation with him about how stupid that was. How do you have that conversation? Here he is doing something that's sweet and nice, but you have to tell him he was being stupid.

That is the problem with this foolishness, this war. The insurgents would use a situation like that. They would get a bunch of kids and then "Boom!" I honestly never worried much about myself. The only thing I cared about was I did not want to write a letter to anyone's parents about how great they were and how unfair it was that they were not coming back anymore. I went with 49, and I wanted to come back with 49.

The war kicked off in March, but it was still the new beginnings of the war when we got there. The infrastructure was almost nonexistent. The airfield we had was nine miles west of Fallujah. It was an old Iraqi air base that had been bombed to smithereens. About 133 bombs were dropped in that airfield. There was an incredible amount of Iraqi ordnance that was strewn all over the base. We were trying to establish operations. It was a huge cleanup to restore it for our use. It was an incredible challenge. We were an air traffic control unit in an airfield none of us had been to, and we were trying to do this within nine miles of Fallujah, which turned into one helluva theater area.

Sometime in early October, we started experiencing mortar attacks, three or four times a week, generally at night until 3 A.M. intermittently. They fired three rounds and ran. We had equipment that showed us if a shot was fired, where it came from. But they were gone by the time we got there.

In late October, a Chinook was shot down. It was a Sunday. There wasn't anything going on. It was our down day, just "allowing soldiers to power down" day. I got a call that two aircraft had just taken off. Two Chinooks just took off doing normal transportation between locations in Iraq, carrying people. They both called in all clear, and then two to three minutes later, the second aircraft came on the radio and said their sister aircraft was shot down. Because my guys controlled the tower, I was one of the first to know, and that started a whole chain of folks being notified. It went from a quiet day to a day of damn. That was the first actual loss of life that we were involved in there. We lost 24 to 25 soldiers in a matter of seconds. It was hard. I called my wife and let her know that I wasn't involved in it. Unfortunately, it was 10 P.M. my time, but it was 2 her time. I'm at war and the phone rings in the middle of the night, and she goes haywire. It was good though because the next time she woke up it was the big thing in the news. Even though I wasn't flying, you never know. It was a bad day but not the only one.

Kimberly Hampton was the first female aviator shot down. I had a chance to meet her two days prior to her being shot down. Our only interaction was negative. There was an aircraft accident involving one of her pilots in command. I had to investigate it, so we got into an argument. About two days later, I found out she was shot down and killed, and the only memory is of a heated fight. I'm sure she was a competent and extraordinary individual. It's hard. . . . Days like that sound crazy, but what do you do? She was shot down and killed outside of Fallujah.

I was also there when the medevac chopper was shot down. Eleven were killed on that one. This was just a week before Kimberly was killed. The night of Kimberly's memorial service, a mortar hit the sleeping area of the commander. It went through the window and blew it apart. But her unit was at the memorial. If it wasn't for that, more people would have been killed.

We were dealing with an overly committed, overly devoted enemy. The insurgents are cowardly sons of bitches. Anytime you have an enemy that doesn't want to make itself known, who hides behind the innocent, behind schools, mosques, anywhere, they know that we, as American people, would refuse to attack them. We soldiers operating in Iraq, we can't tell who are insurgents and who are civilians. It makes it extremely difficult to pick the right from the wrong. It is difficult for soldiers trying to do the right thing. We have never been in this kind of environment. It is unlike anywhere except Vietnam, but even in Vietnam, there was a discernable enemy. The insurgents have done everything possible to harm and kill the innocent, and that is cowardly.

I'm not happy about being in Iraq. But having been there and done that, it's clear we would have been done so long ago if we had an enemy we could see.

Your normal day could be absolutely boring, mundane BS, but in a moment, something happens, and your whole day is screwed up. It's crazy and hard to understand. I didn't want to be there. I didn't choose this war, but as long as I am in the military, that's my job. I am not going to lie and say that I was not fortunate to be part of it. My wish would have been for the war to never have happened. But I would hate to be a major and never have experienced war. I would hate to be a leader who tells people to go out and do things that I have never experienced. Now I have a real perspective on the hardship people are going through. I know the pain of being away from home. I know what it's like to be in a room with six guys, a room the size of 10 by 12 feet; that was our bedroom, operations room, our office—everything you can think of, that room became. I know what it's like to be in war.

Hell, when I came home, things were great. My wife had talked about it before. I didn't want the kids to know. Getting you to the war is easy, but getting you back home is always a problem So I didn't want to tell them I was coming home but instead, just let them know when I got home.

When I got home from Iraq, it was a school day. We went up to the school and surprised each one of my daughters. My wife and I went to the guidance counselor's office at my older daughter's school and had them call her in for a silly reason. She walked right in, past me, in her own world, and I tapped her on the shoulder. It took her a second. It was like she was thinking, "Am I seeing who I think I'm seeing?" Then she broke down. We did the same thing for my younger daughter. She was eating lunch in the cafeteria. I came up behind her and asked, "What are you eating?" And she said, "Peanut butter and jelly." Then she looked at me and lost it. No feeling like that ever. I was happy to be with my family, and they were happy that I was home. Hell, life was great.

I have been back to the area two other times for short periods of time, but I go to Kuwait.

One thing about deployment, you see how good things are here. It is very hard for me to not understand that the average American has so many more opportunities available to them than the average Mexicans, Hondurans, and Iraqis throughout the world. We have things a lot better than other people in the world, and I know that. I've seen it.

DAVE BISCHEL

National Guard Specialist
Lives: Clearlake, California
Iraq War Service: March 2003–April 2004

Before 9/11, I was doing outside wireless communication sales and always feeling that there was something missing in my life. But 9/11 changed a lot of people's lives and how they view their lives, including me. After 9/11, I started reevaluating my priorities. I wanted to be able to help if something bad happened in the West Coast, so I joined the guard. I wanted to be available to help out in a natural disaster. I was in the army full-time from 1989 to 1993. I went back in January 2003 about 10 years after I left. When I went to talk to the recruiter, he told me the military police company that I was going in was getting involved in something big. But he gave me the impression that I would be left in the rear. I was out of shape and had just enlisted, but the next thing I knew, I was on my way to Iraq.

From that point on, I put on my best face, but I had to leave my wife, my daughter, who was 10, and a baby son. We are a pretty liberal family, very few Republicans we have any respect for, but one was Colin Powell. I believed him and what he said about the war. So I went in just thinking that I would try to be as humble and respectful as I could be and let the Iraqi people know that we are all not warmongers and that we know they had sisters, brothers, moms, kids, and fathers.

My first four weeks there, we didn't have bulletproof vests. We had old radio equipment. At times, we were attacked, and we were unable to call for support. Our first five months in Iraq, we were doing patrols. We did raids. We kicked in doors. We were supposed to be training Iraqi police, but it was a joke. They were extremely corrupt, and the people have so much fear of the Iraqi police because under Saddam, they would take people's wives and daughters and murder and rob them, so that was a problem. We had this Iraqi police outfit that was not trained. We had someone running it whom, two weeks ago, was in the police academy. A K-Mart security guard is better trained then the Iraqi police.

I saw a lot of what was considered police brutality. [The Iraqis] would pull people out of cars and start beating people. When we conducted raids, there was no respect between police and people. Numerous people would tell us the Iraqi police were corrupt and robbed and raped people. That was the biggest mistake we did by completely disbanding the Iraqi army. We had to try and put together a ragtag police force. In these little tiny cities, everyone knows everyone. There was a lot of fear of neighbors retaliating against the new police. Some of the high-ranking police people were there for years under Saddam. We would find a few good ones, and they would receive pressure from the colonels not to work with us. It was really hard, and there were so many problems. It was hard to protect the ones that want to work.

We did the best we could, and then our time just kept getting extended, and morale dropped. When we first got there, we were treated like rock stars. "Good President Bush, Saddam bad, Saddam donkey," but then it changed. They'd say they were glad we got rid of Saddam, but then say, "By the way, do you support Israel?"

When we got to Abu Ghraib prison, we were sitting ducks over there all the time.

We monitored the outside walls and who came and left the prison. Another platoon guarded the inside of the prison. The prison was huge, a monster. I was surprised how big it is. It's a prison within a prison. It's huge, and then inside, you have these little smaller prisons. The walls were falling down. Trash piled up everywhere, rusty toilets didn't work, and bugs all over the place. The odor was terrible. Everything was dirty. We had bug bite competition, like, "You show me yours, and I'll show you mine." We had bites all over our bodies. It was insane, and we were hot and sweating all the time.

We were there when the prison abuse took place, but we didn't see any of it. We worked 12-hour days with no days off for four months. Watching the news, we'd hear them say we have plenty of troops, but we were wondering where they were because we didn't see them.

✶　✶　✶

One time, when I was up in the tower doing a 12-hour shift, a ranger unit came up to do surveillance. One of the captains said, "You don't have to lie to me. I know you fell asleep." I told him, "You are absolutely right."

Our company as a whole killed quite a few Iraqis. The majority of the firefights were them taking potshots at us, and by the time we figured out where they were coming from, they were gone.

We caught four guys once. These guys, who were 100 meters behind us, opened fire with AK-47s. We had no idea where they were coming from. Then we figured it out and chased them into a building. They were the Iraqi security force who were supposed to be guarding a gas station. We handed out new AK-47s to Iraqi police, and it was these guards who were trying to kill us. Luckily none of our guys were killed.

People started having psychological problems. For pain, they give you 800 milligrams of Motrin. But for psychological problems,

they started handing out Prozac and Paxil. Their attitude was, suck it up. There was a point in Abu Ghraib, I didn't realize it, but I just started deteriorating mentally. I was like, "Fuck Iraq. I want to kill these motherfuckers and go home." You get to the point you lose it. It's like, "Fuck it, fuck them. They don't want us here." It drove me crazy. When you try to talk to people, they say, "Why did you sign up? What did you think would happen?" They lose sight of how this war happened. You don't send troops in harm's way unless it's absolutely necessary. You shouldn't be sent away for some bullshit. People lose focus on the human component of being a soldier in harm's way. When you are told you are only go to be there for six months, and it keeps getting extended, and you watch the death toll go up, it does something to you. I remember when we saw it close in on 500; now we are over 2,000. My wife got very concerned about it.

It got to the point where I was being ostracized because I started questioning what was going on. I wrote a letter to my congressman that was read on the floor. I would find articles I wrote with degrading comments on them. But some would say, "Right on, Bischel." But I didn't care. I wanted to come home. When I left Iraq, I took the Prozac they gave me, and I became very outspoken. Everywhere I went, I had cameras in my face.

The hardest thing when I came home was whenever I heard a loud noise, it would freak me out. We went to Disneyland, and they did a fireworks display, and when they started going off, I hit the floor. My daughter hit the ground, too. I started looking for my weapon. I was freaked out. It took me awhile to not freak out when a car backfired. It was kind of tough.

I was in the guard for 16 months, and I was supposed to do 12. They put pressure on us to reenlist, but I felt totally exploited. I was a bullet catcher. No freaking way was I going to reenlist. I'd rather shovel cow manure. It was so obvious to me when I came back that it was amazing that anyone can support this war. They should be seeing the coffins coming back, the families in tears. They lost sight of the component that we are human beings killing other human beings.

The war is based on lies. You remember the way Kenneth Starr[1] went after Clinton? All that money spent, and Clinton just lied about an affair. He didn't kill anybody. Who knows how many Iraqis have been killed. Where is Kenneth Starr now? It's all freaking insane.

---

[1]Independent counsel who investigated President Bill Clinton while he was in the White House.

MATTHEW MILLER

National Guard Sergeant

Lives: Pasadena, Maryland

Iraq War Service: February 2005–present

(This interview was conducted while Sgt. Miller was serving in Iraq.)

Humans are extremely adaptive and very good at causing acute pain and suffering to other humans. We are very good at making war.

I fly medevac in Black Hawk helicopters in Iraq. I've had five soldiers die in the back of my 'copter. I still remember their names, and I don't forget their faces. And those are just the ones that I know have died. It's extremely exhausting and depressing. You do the best you can with the tools and skills that you have, and it doesn't always work. I'm lucky I have a good wife at home. I call her every night. She is my sounding board.

I had a young African American guy—I think he was 27. He was a truck driver. What happened was the humvee in front of him blew up, and a piece of shrapnel came in from the window of the tractor-trailer he was driving and hit him on the side of the head. No one else was hurt.

When we landed out there in the desert, I could tell he was hurt bad. The soldiers were breathing for him. We loaded him in the aircraft and just continued breathing for him and got him on an EKG. His heart rate was only 30 beats per minute. It was bad. My crew chief started CPR, and I intubated him, which means I inserted a tube down his throat. I got his airway secure, and his heart rate went up, and some of the problems started to get better. He was still unconscious, but my hopes were getting high. The wound on his head was bandaged, so we continued to monitor him and gave him some fluids to try and nudge his pressure up. Then his head wound started bleeding, and the bandage came loose. When I tried to adjust it, brain matter started coming out of the hole. I was just watching his life spiraling down. It was like putting a house of cards together, and it tumbles down.

We did CPR again, and he went into trauma arrest. We took him to CSH [combat support hospital], and they never quit on this kid. The commander was there, and I'm watching them work on this guy. I just knew he was going to die by what I saw. His commander was a young captain, and he was just sitting there crying. There were probably 30 people there. They weren't saying anything, just watching.

They finally called it . . . you could have heard a pin drop in that place. I gathered my things. I was really upset. I got back in the helicopter, and the pilot was like, "Let's get gas." I said, "Let's just go home." It took 20 minutes to clean the blood out of the aircraft. Afterward, I looked like I aged 20 years.

I had trouble sleeping after that. He was a big, muscular guy, 6'2". I still remember his face and name—James.

We ran a mission two weeks ago. People were working in the old pipeline; the insurgents saw them working, and they set a land mine at the entrance. An Iraqi worker walked in, and it blew up. One guy had a piece of shrapnel that flew up his back and took out his lung. It was a lot of work, but I saved him. His blood was just coming out of the hole and sprayed all over. I was able to get the hole covered and got his lung inflated.

You never really think about how it wears you down. We came back from that and I took a short nap. At about 10:30 that night, we got a call that an IED [improvised explosive device] hit a gun truck and detonated it, so we launched. While we were en route, we could hear over the radio the ground crew talking. One of the guys had died.

We landed. It was really creepy, a lot of smoke. We approached their ground medic. You could hear in their voices, they are all keyed up. The ground medic, he was working on one young kid, about 19. Shrapnel had torn through his right leg, then his left leg, and blew part of his right hand off. It blew three of five fingers off. Their interpreter was killed. The shrapnel that went through the interpreter then hit the kid. I'm talking to the kid, and he is hurting, but he is trying to be a tough guy. The medic was telling me he had no morphine, and then this weird thing happens. This guy walks out of the smoke and grabs me by the vest. A piece of shrapnel went flying through his nose. It practically took it off. He said, "Don't worry about me. Take care of my soldiers." I asked him to come with me, and he said, "No, I'm riding with my soldiers." He then turned around and walked away into the smoke and disappeared.

I got the kid in the 'copter and took care of him. It is so strange. I was sound asleep one second, and next thing you know I'm going to pick up a kid who an hour ago was full of life, but it kills you. You get to save a lot of them, but you see a lot of kids with missing arms and legs. I had one kid, shrapnel took both his legs. He was bleeding so bad, and man, I could not stop it. He even had tourniquets on his leg. His pressure dropped, and I'm worried he is going to bleed to death.

What you see the most is head trauma and a lot of arms and legs missing. When the IEDs blow up, it tears up everything it goes through.

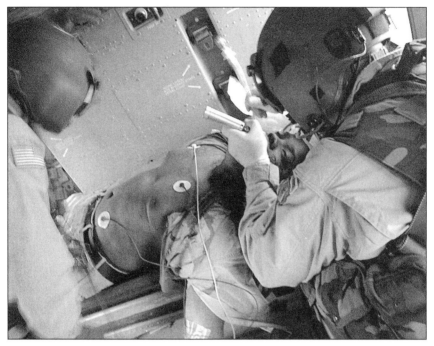

© Thomas Dworzak/Magnum Photo

* * *

I'm a firefighter back home, a paramedic. I run about 1,000 calls a year, which is a lot. About 40 of them are big; the rest are just BS. Here I've run five years of multisystem trauma patients in five months, and they don't stop coming. I have flown 2,030 hours and evacuated about 300 soldiers.

At home it's car crashes, but their body parts are still on them. Here there is so much blood and pieces of bodies missing. We have sprayed out our aircrafts and have found pieces of bone. The injuries are anything from extremely minor, to shrapnel, burns, and gunshot wounds. It's a 24-hour operation. I spend 72 straight hours on call, and then I get a day off and back again. It is extremely tiring. I'm 37.

Everyone wants to be politically correct, but it's important that people see and hear what really goes on. Some of these kids are doing great work. They have a lot of heart. It pains me to see it minimized by the news. Only the sensational gets reported. You hear 30 Iraqis killed by a suicide bomber, but the one private that got killed in the humvee, you don't hear about. That happens a lot.

Most of us believe in what we are doing, and most Iraqis are happy that we are here. You see kids playing soccer and people going back to work. The people were being brutalized. They are ecstatic that we are here, which is cool. But still, some kids throw rocks at you. You help the majority and try and suppress the ones that are starting trouble.

I'm the senior flight personnel. I'm also the combat stress control NCO [noncommissioned officer]. We had one soldier who is not flying anymore. He flew out, picked up a young woman who took shrapnel that perforated her heart. It bothered him bad. I talked to him for three hours that night. He was never able to bounce back.

I just reenlisted for another six years. I like being an army guy, but I'm looking forward to being a fireman again. I got 12 years in now. It would be foolish to leave. I'm hoping I don't have to come back to Iraq. I'm a flight instructor. I'm very good at teaching, so I hope to head out to pasture and be nondeployable.

I don't want to cry until I get home. If I'm going to tell people back home what is going on, the most important thing I want to do is tell it real.

DR. TRACEY RINGO

National Guard Major
Lives: Cleveland, Ohio
Iraq War Service: July 2004–October 2004

People ask me, "What do you think about the war?" "Should we be there?" And my answer is, "We are there whether we should or shouldn't be, and we need to finish what we started." I believe we need to help the Iraqis and then bring our troops home, but I think it's going to be like Germany and Korea. We are always going to have troops stationed there.

I feel great about what I did. It's the best work I have ever done. I know why I was there, and it was very fulfilling.

* * *

I joined the National Guard in the fall of 1988. I went in as a medic because I always knew I wanted to be a doctor. By the time I went into medical school, I was already doing a lot of things that other students had not done. In the military, you have more freedom in terms of practice, and so I could train and do sutures and help set fractures—things in the civilian world, you couldn't do unless you have that certification.

I was in throughout Desert Storm but was not activated, just on standby. So when Iraqi Freedom started, I figured, more or less, we wouldn't be going. Our first issue here is to make sure the troops here are ready and get them medically certified to go over there. That was our mission. But the rules changed. They said we needed doctors, and though our unit wasn't affected as a whole, they pulled all the doctors in the unit to fill spots in Iraq. I was supposed to go in the fall of 2004, but one guy found out his wife was having a baby, and I wound up filling it for him and going July of 2004.

* * *

A couple of weeks before I left, they captured Saddam. The climate was changing when I got there. I knew I was going. I wasn't fearful. I just concentrated on coming back home. I wanted a clear mind, and I knew I had to do my job. I also relied on my faith. I kept saying, "I know the Lord hasn't brought me this far to leave me." I must have said that a thousand times.

People did not smile there, but my nickname was "Smiley." I made a vow to myself that I would not have any negative vibes over there. I needed to be positive and be an inspiration to someone. You know, I'm wearing the medical uniform, and I'm going to see people that are hurt and discouraged and need a positive attitude.

* * *

I was the palace physician stationed in the Green Zone,[1] which was then at the presidential palace. It was a beautiful palace. It had a pool, commodes made of gold, marble sidewalks. Saddam was living the life. I guess there were at least 50 bathrooms. But we didn't live in the palace; we lived on the grounds in a trailer.

I was the senior officer, with a physician's assistant and six medics working under me. We were in charge of day-to-day medical care of troops, setting up a mass casualty plan and Emergency Medical Services. We were also the only clinic in the theater [i.e., war zone] that took care of Iraqi citizens.

I was on 24-hour call seven days a week. We had a lot of calls at two and three in the morning. It was a very physical job; I did a lot of running. The palace was huge.

It was not safe. It gave you the illusion of being safe, but it wasn't. About 5,000 Iraqis lived within the zone. The compound had its on security, but they would fire from across the river into the compound. We were hit with mortars a lot. I lived in a trailer, but we had bunkers we went to when we were attacked. We got bombed a lot at night. One time, in a three-day period, we were bombed all

---

[1]A heavily guarded area where U.S. occupation authorities work and live, now known as the International Zone.

night from 10 P.M. to 3 A.M. Then I prayed the longest prayer I ever had. I said, "Lord, I can't take this, not one more night." We had 6 bombs one night; another night, 11. People were saying tonight would be 15, and I said, "No, I prayed about this." That night there were none. There was no place that was safe, no job that was safe. It wasn't like we were doing hand-to-hand combat, but these rockets and mortars were being fired at us.

It was loud. If someone told you it was hitting five miles away, you felt they were lying. It felt more like five feet away. The force of the explosions was powerful. People got so they could tell if it was a car bomb, mortar, or whatever going off.

*　*　*

The palace, while I was there, was hit twice. It was a target. It was headquarters, and all the high-ranking officials were there. Once a bomb hit, and the ceiling came down on a lady at her desk. I had to crawl through a patio ledge to get to her, and it was small. I'm 5'2", 127 pounds, and it came in handy. We also had a lot of bombs that came in as unidentified packages, and then the bomb unit would come in. They would call us and tell us they found a suspicious package, and the bomb unit would be here to detonate. So everyone had to evacuate and get far away, except for me. They'd say, "I need you right here." I was a little disturbed by that. We were going through the crowd, and everyone was consolidated a couple of miles away, but they wanted us up close and personal. I was like, "What is wrong with this?"

One day, the guy who detonated the bombs had this big suit on, but maybe he wasn't drinking his water, and he was getting hot and dehydrated. He asked for one of us to start an IV while he has this suit on and is working on the bomb. I said it was not a reasonable request. You can't start an IV with your suit on and detonate a bomb with us standing there. We'd be way too close to that bomb. But the guy who detonates the bombs is very important. If he wants a steak dinner while working, he gets one right away. I told them if he feels dehydrated, he should drink some water while he worked.

We had some strange requests, and I had to put my foot down. You know, our medical unit needed to be safe, too. If we all got hurt, who was going take care of everybody?

✲ ✲ ✲

One day, we had a family of four going into our checkpoint, and the father blew up the car. They all died except one of the children. He lived, and he had missing limbs. He wound up at the hospital without a family, fighting for his life. You would think, "Oh, this is safe. This man has his family with him." But his whole focus was getting to this checkpoint and blowing it up. How do you fight someone like that?

The child was about six or seven. It was hard. I don't know if that child made it or not.

✲ ✲ ✲

There was this nice outdoor market right across the street from the palace we all went to, Iraqi citizens and us. It was a place we would go to mingle, but 90 percent of the people that would go there were troops. Three individuals strapped themselves to a bomb and blew it up. The marketplace was blown up. There was a lot of death—people burnt to death, women and children, and there was nothing you could do. It was Ramadan, and everything started heating up. We were told to stay away from certain areas, and it happened around when the market would be full. It was right across the street from the palace. They didn't get as many people as they would have if we didn't have the intelligence. The market used to be 90 percent full with the troops. After that, we were in lockdown. We couldn't leave the compound.

✲ ✲ ✲

I had a translator so I could communicate with the Iraqi people and an Iraqi medical student. The people wanted to see us. Just to get advice from an American doctor for them was great. The

Iraqis worked in the Green Zone and in the presidential palace, so we'd see seizure, headaches, dehydration, fractures, everything. A lot of them were fasting throughout the day. They wouldn't drink water, and they would pass out. We were drinking water like crazy, and they were fasting.

The people were humble and very grateful that we were there. It was not like what I saw on the news. They wanted us there. The overall feeling we got was that they were so happy that we were there.

There was a song my interpreter would sing about the American invasion, about the American troops coming to save them. She would sing it all the time, and she was so grateful that we were there. Saddam himself ran her family out of Baghdad.

She said you could not let your neighbors know that you were working for the Americans. Not even her family knew. They didn't know where she was going or what she was doing. When she came to my work, she had one outfit on, and then she would change into something else so she couldn't be tracked.

✳ ✳ ✳

I struggled about coming back to the States. I felt like I was leaving my team. They changed the law for the National Guard doctors after Desert Storm. During that war, a doctor had to serve for a year. But after their stint was over, they didn't have a practice left when they came back, and they lost everything. Your patients can't wait a year, so they would find another doctor. So those doctors had to leave the guard. This new law was so they could keep the doctors in the military. We do only 90-day rotations.

I even had to talk to the military psychologist. I had been questioning if I wanted to come at all, and then I didn't want to leave. He said it's time for me to go and that I did my time. He said the longer you stay, it gets harder to leave.

When I came home, I didn't know how I would be, but I put it behind me and don't talk about it much. My family doesn't ask me.

I'm still in the guard. Right now, going back—that's on the table. I'm due to go back soon. We'll see. I'm married now, and I have a nine-month-old son.

* * *

I get emotional before a basketball game now. The flag means so much more to me than it ever did before. I've always been patriotic, but even more so now. A lot of people have lost their lives for that flag to fly, and when I see it, I think about them. I am grateful for them.

ROBERT ACOSTA

Army Specialist

Lives: Santa Ana, California

Iraq War Service: April 2003–July 2003

I joined the army for a few reasons. I wasn't doing well in high school, so I dropped out. I was working little jobs, whatever, using drugs and stuff. I was going nowhere fast and just wanted to get out. There were no opportunities, and I didn't want to go to school. I didn't even want to finish high school. It was boring. You could tell the teacher didn't care, and I got discouraged. I good friend of mine had just come back from boot camp, and he was talking about it. I wasn't doing anything, and so that's why I joined.

I signed up when I was 17, in October of 2000, but I had to wait because I had to get my GED. I finally got that, then had to wait some more. I left for boot camp in August 2001, a month before 9/11. I was 18.

After 9/11, I was like, "Shit, we're going to war." We flew into Kuwait City in April 2003. Things had seemed to be dying down; they were saying it was the end of the war. I was an ammunition specialist and was finally doing the job I was trained for. I was stationed at Baghdad Airport and the area surrounding it. We mostly had indirect fire, a rocket here and there. It wasn't like a shootout type of thing.

I didn't care about Iraq. I was in the army. We were just focused on doing what I had to do and then going home. When we were in Kuwait, soldiers were passing out left and right because there wasn't enough water. We had to go to other units and steal their water. Once we got to Iraq, it was even worse; the water wasn't coming in. They'd bring us a big thing of water, and they said it was safe to drink and then changed their minds. We had bottles that were open already and broken. They had a water tower at the airport but said the water wasn't any good. We had to drive off from the airport to get water. It was really unorganized. I didn't get my body armor until a week before I got injured. We had old flak vests. They then gave us new ones, but they didn't have plates. We made our own armor with cans. We'd flatten them out. You get mad, but there is nothing you can do about it. You can't bitch to your chain of command because they would tell you just deal with it, so you just dealt with it.

The day I got injured was my day off. I was hanging out. The fire department would fill these big concrete holes in the ground with water, and we'd go swimming. So my friend and I went swimming with some other friends, and we were having a good time. Afterward, we decided to go out and pick up some stuff for my soldiers. We asked an E7 [first sergeant] for a humvee, and he said, "Yeah, but only if you buy some stuff for me." And he gave me some money. We were going to buy sodas and ice, which is like gold out there.

So we go and drive out, past the airport, and on to the airport road, which was called "IED [improvised explosive device] alley," and the neighborhood of Abu Ghraib. I had this guy I would always go to. It was legit, and we'd always buy from him. But my friend would always buy from someone else because he was in a different company. His guy was further down the road than what I was used to. As we drove, we both kind of noticed there was no military presence. We were the only humvee in this neighborhood, and I was like, "Fuck this. Let's make a U-turn and go back." People were starting to come out of their houses and staring at us. We tried to get back onto the airport road, but then the car in front of us stopped, and then there were people standing on each side of the vehicle. All of a sudden through my window, which was open, I see it—a grenade was thrown into our vehicle, between the driver's seat and me. I grabbed it. I knew what it was. I grabbed it with my right hand and threw it out, but I fucking dropped it back in the humvee. I reached down again and grabbed it, and it popped. I almost got it out. My hand was gone automatically. My leg was all fucked up. I was still conscious. My friend didn't get hurt at all. We started shooting. I tried to fire a round. It was the first time I'd fired a gun in Iraq. So there is this car in front of us; people are yelling. It's fucking chaos, dude. I'm like, "Let's get the fuck out of here." I put my hand out the window because I don't want to see it. My friend hits it, pushes about three or four cars out of the way, and he is running people over. We get on the airport road, and there are more and more people there. Someone on the divider tries to flag us down, and my friend made a sharp left and took him out, and that guy was literally right in front me on the car all messed up.

There were so many people, and they were all after us. It was fucking crazy. We were in traffic just knocking people off the road. My friend is yelling at me, "You'll be all right." At that point, I was, like, fucked. I said, "Tell my family I'm sorry." I was in no pain. He is yelling at me to stay awake, but I was so up, I remember every detail.

I started getting dizzy, and I thought, "This is it. I am dying in this shithole." We finally got out of there and hauled ass on the airport road. The vehicle died at the gate of an air force base. My friend gets out and says, "Don't worry. You'll be fine." He runs over to that gate and tells them I'm hurt. He comes back, picks me up because my legs are broken, and throws me on his back. He then carries me to the gate and tells the guys to take me to the hospital.

The whole time I was cursing out the air force guys who took me to the hospital. One guy was trying to hold my hand. I wanted water, and they wouldn't give it to me. I wanted a cigarette. Those guys got a Bronze Star for driving me two minutes to the airport. My friend got nailed. They said that it was his fault we went out there. He got 45 days' extra duty without pay. They said it was our fault. The E-7 who gave us the vehicle said we just took it, which was a lie. I was put in for a Bronze Star, but it was rejected.

My leg sucks; it's messed up. They almost had to cut it off. There was a big hole in my leg, like two inches.

In Baghdad, they told me my hand's gone, but the doctor said he was going to try and save my leg. I lost a lot of blood. I was really mad. I was yelling at everybody. My legs above my knee took a lot of shrapnel. Every time they moved me, my leg hurt so much. My hand never hurt.

They sent me to Walter Reed Hospital. I was there for seven months. I hated it, but the nurses and doctors are amazing. I don't even know how many surgeries I had. It seemed like every week, I was having a couple of surgeries. My throat was real sore because they had to put a tube down my throat each time.

I didn't want to live anymore. I was done. I was 20 years old and all fucked up. I was really depressed; I didn't want to do anything. They told me I needed to be on antidepressants, but I didn't want to take them. I'd get really frustrated. I really wanted to kill myself. I just didn't know how. It was a hard time. I was really unhappy. I would cry. I couldn't sleep at night. I still can't sleep for shit. I feel really antsy all the time. It's weird—at night, I'm paranoid. I sleep with a gun by me. It's with me wherever I go. It's not normal. It just sucks. It's hard, dude. I feel I got caught sleeping one time, and it ain't going to happen again.

The president came twice, and I left. I didn't want to meet him. I feel he and his whole administration lies and puts our lives in jeopardy. He didn't want to meet me.

I went home in January 2004. I had the whole hero's welcome ceremony at the courthouse, and that was cool and everything. The spotlight was on me. When I got hurt, my girlfriend, who was my friend, then got a hold of me, and we started talking. She was very supportive. If it weren't for her, I wouldn't be here. Still, sometimes, I'm like, "Why am I here?" She is always there to tell me otherwise. So I was really close to her when I got home. I clung to her.

My girlfriend is in college, and she went to study in Spain. I started drinking and taking pills. I would drink all day long, all night. Sometimes I wouldn't sleep, just drink and take pills. I needed to get away from that. I had money saved up and met her in Spain. We went to nine countries, and I stopped the pills.

I was going to school for a while, but it was hard being home and doing normal everyday shit. I feel like such an outcast. I didn't feel I fit into society, and I get depressed because of it. At school, everyone was staring at me, and people were always asking about my hand. Sometimes, it's too much. I went this semester. I went to all my classes for one day, had a fight with my girlfriend, and then dropped out. I stress out too easily.

I don't wear the electric prosthetic. It's heavy, it makes you sweat, and then it slides off. It's really uncomfortable. I really liked the hook. It was easier to use. I got so mad one day at Walter Reed, I threw the prosthetic against the wall. I hate that stupid thing. I wear the hook when I play pool, but it draws more attention. I'm more comfortable without it.

I had a fake hand, too. I wore that a lot for a while. It was light. If I wore a long-sleeved shirt, you couldn't tell. Then a finger broke off of it, and I had it taped up with safety pins, and it looked really ghetto. To get another, I'd have to deal with the VA, and I can't deal with it.

The VA fucked me over. They sent me a letter telling me my claims were denied for my leg and PTSD [posttraumatic stress disorder], my hearing, and a lot of shit. They said nothing was wrong with my leg. I flipped out. I have a bar in my leg. I have a lot of ringing in my ears. Sometimes I can't hear; sometimes it's fine. They tried to say my leg would get better, but it's gotten worse. I don't like crowds. I almost crashed my car because I was seeing things on the road. My other hand hurts because I overuse it. I was wigging out. Not getting my benefits cost me $500 just on bounced checks. Then the *Washington Post* called me, and I told them everything. The article comes out, and the next day, the chief of staff of the VA called me. I told her I couldn't even live. Then the next day I got a check. Two weeks later, I get this check in the mail and a letter that says they bump up my rating from 100 percent to 120 percent disabled. A few weeks later, they bumped it up to 200 percent because of the PTSD.

I go every Wednesday for therapy, but I mostly go to be with the guys. It doesn't help one bit, but afterward, we all hang out and smoke cigarettes outside. That's all I do with the VA.

I had a job for a while when I got back doing fiber optic cable splicing. The guy I worked for even wanted to send me to school. But he was a born-again Christian, and he was trying so hard to convert me, and I couldn't deal with having a job and the responsibility.

I liked being in the army until Iraq. I was a really good soldier. I did everything I was told. Every now and then, I go to the list and see who died. I'll see people's names that I know. It's sad, man.

MARK MITCHELL

National Guard Specialist
Lives: Philadelphia, Pennsylvania
Iraq War Service: April 2003–December 2003

I joined the military in March of 1982, did six years, and left because it was racist. I wasn't being treated right. I rejoined in August 1990. I wanted to drive trucks, and that's why I went back. A few months later, I was mobilized for Desert Storm. It wasn't as bad as this go-around. We were dealing with a lot of Scuds flying overhead. You heard airplanes going over you and dropping bombs. I was there from January to late March, but my father passed away, so I left early. I got out in 1993 and then I reenlisted to drive trucks again. I was a prison guard, I had a state job, but I was looking at the money and benefits.

Life was normal up until 2003. I was mobilized in January to go to Iraq. I knew what had to be done. My big problems were going over there and being with people who didn't know what had to be done. I had more experience in the chow hall than some of these people had in the army. I was 38.

I was in the mostly black part of the unit. The other units were white. One guy told me he never seen a black person before, so you can imagine what we were up against. There was a little racism. The leaders had favorites, and the detach part was not one of them, but most of the guys were good guys. My job was to transport equipment and supplies in Iraq. We had one job with Motorola, where we hauled millions of dollars of Motorola equipment.

When I first got to Iraq, there was a guy who found a piece of old artillery, and he picked it up, and he and another guy started playing with it like a baseball. One night I was asleep, and from what I gathered, the explosive went off. The guy had it lying in a footlocker in front of his bed, and he and another guy were doing some horseplay, and they hit it, and it blew up. Part of one guy's leg was blown off. The guy who found the artillery caught metal in his head, and another guy hurt his back and lost his hearing. Before you go in there, they tell if you don't know what it is, don't pick it up. They said he showed it to his safety officer, and the officer said he didn't know what it was, but he didn't confiscate it.

We had a lot of sniper fire, and two RPGs [rocket-propelled grenades] just missed my truck one night. The guy in charge of that mission was a sergeant first class, and he was a total prick. I didn't like him. You couldn't tell him nothing. He figured he got the rank, he is in charge, so you have to do what he says.

It was getting dark, and they called brown-out condition. It's almost dark, and it's sandy, and we couldn't see anything. The road was like 15 feet wide, so you are not turning a tractor-trailer around. You had a lot of guys saying, "Go this way. Go this way." He decided to go another way, and it almost cost some lives. I had just seen out of the corner of my eye a red flare. Then I heard a boom and then a shot right across the roof of my truck. It must have been two guys because another shot just missed the back of it.

In those situations, you are trained to just move out. But the NCO [noncommissioned officer] said, "Hit the brake," and we stalled. We just became sitting targets. So my partner and me were not too happy with him. We are hollering on the radio that we are getting shot at. We were lucky no one was hurt.

Prior to that, we were already in a sniper situation. The NCO didn't know where he was going, so he is turning us all around in Baghdad. A truck was losing cargo, and we pulled over to secure it, and the next thing you know, we're being fired at. So we moved out of there. We all wanted to go to this certain area where we knew we would be safe, but he didn't want to, and that's what happened.

Some bitter feelings were going on there, and I chose to go on no more missions with him. My feeling is I might not outrank you, but I have a lot of experience running trucks, tying down loads. But he couldn't take my experience into consideration and listen to what I was trying to tell him. All he could see was rank and structure. I could have shot that guy myself that night. A lot of the leadership was kind of incompetent to me, and that made it stressful.

Sometimes, someone got a flat tire or something, and you'd have to pop out of your truck and take a defensive position. What pissed me off about that is there would be other people who were in their trucks taking a damn nap. That kind of stuff would piss you off. They'd tell you things like if you go to a certain place, you need to be in a certain type of uniform, and then you have guys who wouldn't do it. You had a lot of guys who took some things for granted, but I wasn't one.

I trusted no Iraqi. I barely trusted the children. You can't trust any of them. To me they smile in your face in the day, then shoot at you at night. In the daytime, they are all out there. They want to sell you this or that, all smiling, but when night falls, all you hear is a bunch of shooting. They'd come up to my truck. I'd tell them to get away. They were always trying to sell you things. If they didn't understand me, I'd put the muzzle to their face and say go. I didn't trust them. They are suicidal. You never know. They walk you to your truck; the next thing you know, you are blowing up.

I transported supplies and equipment, air conditioners, food, water, communications stuff, and water. It was boring. There were no billboards to read. If you break down in the desert, suddenly all these people seem to come around you. They'd come out of nowhere, but let me tell you, if you left that truck, I guarantee you that truck would get stripped down to bare metal. They must have had powerless, cordless tools on them because they could strip a truck in a minute—tires, and seats, engines, everything. It was amazing. It being a third world country, they just didn't have equipment like that, but they could sure strip a truck.

You see a body here and there. The first war I saw a lot of bodies charred and burning, that sort of thing, and this sort of awakened a lot of stuff in me. As time went on, I got worse. I started having panic attacks and bad anxiety attacks. It felt like someone was about to push me over a bridge. I had no control over it. It would just happen. When you come back from a mission and find bullet holes in your truck, you're like, "Damn, that just missed me. Look at this hole. Look at where it's at." We'd get shot at a lot. Never knew who was going to ride by, or if your vehicle would blow up or the vehicle in front of you, or who was going to be shooting at you. You'd listen to the radio, hear them say there's sniper fire here or there, look out for guys wearing this or that. Everyone that rides by you, you're pointing a weapon at them waiting to shoot at them. I took it one day at a time. I wasn't sleeping, maybe one or two hours a night. My blood pressure was up, and I didn't trust anybody, not even my own leadership. They were stupid, incompetent, from the captain on down. The captain was a big liar. Whenever she opened her mouth, it was a lie. Why do you speak on us leaving if you don't know when we are leaving? Just say you don't know. Instead, she'd say we were leaving and then deny she'd said it, but the whole company heard it.

I came home. They sent me for a stress test, and I was so stressed-out and nervous that they sent me back to the States for combat stress leave for 90 days. But then it turns out my unit was coming home. I was then medical-boarded out of the guard. To this day, I hear explosions in my sleep.

The hardest thing about this war compared to the first Gulf War was in the Iraq War, I knew more and knew how things should go. I had more confidence in myself. These people wanted things done another way, and they didn't know what they were doing. With a little rank on their shoulders, it was a power struggle. At home, they could have been flipping burgers at McDonald's. But now that had some rank, they would be like, "I'm Mr. Big Shot." My response was "You could shove it up your ass." Also, the people I served with, many of them didn't care. They didn't do the guard duty when they were supposed to. They just thought of themselves.

I don't ever want to go back—hell, no. They can have that country. It was a good thing they took Saddam out of power. I don't know how he slept at night, but I've had enough of the military. I wanted to do 20 years, but I can't do another war.

NATHANIEL J. GANZEVELD

Marine Reserves Corporal

Lives: Dearborn, Michigan

Iraq War Service: February 2003–October 2003

I had my 21st birthday in Iraq. I was among the first marine troops to cross the DMZ [demilitarized zone] from Kuwait and go to Iraq, and it was interesting to be the first one to go in the country. We were an infantry unit providing security for the helicopters when they landed. We were so many times just in the middle of the desert, and whatever was around us, we'd clear it away. The enemy—we didn't call them insurgents then—were always trying to get close to where the helicopters landed. The helicopters were big targets. We were about an hour or so from the borders. I was a basic rifleman. I carried a machine gun most of the time I was in Iraq.

Every day was something new. These troops set up a small base ahead of us, and right before we'd go there, these Iraqis—they had a flatbed truck; they tried to get through the lines there, and as soon as they got near the lines, they slammed on their brakes. Fifteen guys who were in the back jumped off and started shooting, and the guys on the base shot them all. We got there when it had just happened. There was lot of blood and brain matter splattered everywhere.

When you are driving though Iraq, you see dead Iraqis slumped over the steering wheel. You see bullet holes in them because they wouldn't stop for our checkpoints. You know that was the main thing: if they didn't stop, we would go ahead and shoot.

We stopped a lot of vehicles. One time, it was the worst sandstorm in 10 years. You couldn't see your hand in front of your face, but we stopped this vehicle, and there were two guys, Iraqi soldiers with AK-47s and magazines in their vehicles. We weren't taking prisoners, so we took their weapons, ammo, and their shoes. We took the keys to their car and locked it. Then left them on the side of the road.

People were shooting at us all the time. It sounded like snaps or pops over your heads. They were taking potshots at us from rooftops and stuff. It was hard. We were just trying to push our way north. We couldn't shoot back easy because there were women and children around.

We saw so much death and destruction. A lot of it was just crazy. Every day something new would happen. We didn't even have enough food; we would have to steal from other units. The good times were being with the guys, but the bad times, man, it sucked so bad. People were committing suicide who couldn't take it anymore. The last week I was there, someone blew his brains out in the port-o-john on the base. I had a lot of friends who died. A girl from this area, she was killed in a car bombing. Another friend from boot camp was killed. He was shot with an AK-47 in the chest, and it went right up inside him and cut him up. I was in Iraq for eight months.

* * *

I joined the Marine Reserves in the summer of 2000. I was at Henry Ford Community College in Dearborn when 9/11 happened. Part of me was excited when we were called up.

Growing up here, the Arabs are everywhere, but they don't come to this side of town. We have the most Iraqis outside the Middle East here, and the most veterans per capita live in Dearborn.

On this side, mainly the white people live here. Blacks will come into the area. My neighbor is a black marine. We always talk about the Arab people. I'm not a racist, but you know what I mean. You look at when my grandparents grew up—there was so much racial segregation, but it was mainly between the blacks and the whites, and now it's kind of like whites, blacks, Mexicans are against the Arabs. I have friends who are Arabs, but right now there is a lot of tension. When September 11 happened in our city, you could see FBI agents everywhere kicking in doors taking people's computers. I saw them going into Arab people's houses.

* * *

I have posttraumatic stress. Never thought I would have something like that. You can't function. My symptoms didn't show up right away. Then everything just caught up to me and hit me all at once. Overseas there is no time to be scared and frightened, but you experience all this high stress. Then you get home, you relax, and then it just comes rushing up. I have nightmares that I'm back in Iraq watching my dear friend get killed. I still can't sleep. I only sleep four hours a night, that's it, and I'm up. Last night I stayed up until 4:30 A.M. and woke up at 7:30 A.M., and I'll be up all day. It's hard to sleep. Me and my wife, we lay in bed, and I would be violently shaking and sweating, and she'd wake me up.

I'm still fighting to get 100 percent disability. They wrote in my file that I am unable to work, but the way the VA works, once you get 70 to 100 percent, they give you a certificate of unemployability, and I am just 60 percent right now. I have mental and physical problems, and I was diagnosed as having a bad back. They only gave me 10 percent for my back and knee, which I injured in training exercises.

I used to work, and now, I don't know, it's just hard to deal with people, especially in the workplace. I did construction, and I

worked at a pollution control company, cleaning up chemical spills, and I was going to college. We bought a house, and everything was getting paid for, but then I couldn't work. I'd get stressed-out just being at work. I'd get upset, and I'd get into it with the guys. I couldn't hold a job down. The only way I can survive is my wife works. I got kids. We have a daughter, my wife is pregnant, and I have a son who doesn't live with us, and my wife has a son who does.

When I go for my appointments and you see the veterans, the Vietnam vets and World War II vets, they try to pass off info to us. They tell us to tell other vets about the VA, that maybe if they were more involved, they wouldn't shut down our programs or shut us down. When I came home, no one even told me about the VA. It was like, "Oh, you'll be OK." It seems like at a time when the veteran population is building back up again, when you have an influx of people needing these programs, they are being cut. They cut out substance abuse programs and moved them all in with psych ward, and it doesn't make any sense. The program that deals with pain management, they shut that down. They used to have a massage therapist come down, which was beneficial for my back, but then they cut that program out. Why do they keep cutting our programs?

I support the president. I know he has tough decisions to make, but the way that we are treated is not right. I have mixed feelings about the war. I think I would be more supportive of it if they weren't cutting programs for veterans.

I love going to the VA and going to my appointments. I like that the VA hires veterans first, and that's the right thing to do. I enjoy talking to veterans and seeing the familiar faces—that's a good day for me. I take the bus down Michigan Avenue, and I like doing it. Going to the hospital is something I enjoy. Funny, huh? I'm only 22. I still have my friends my age but not on the same level anymore. I like the older guys; those guys are my buddies now. It's weird. I relate to the older veterans more than the kids I grew up with. They understand me. They were there. They know what advice to give me and what helped them.

The way they are cutting VA hospitals and programs makes me feel unappreciated and disposable. It's like they say, "We love you guys. You are America's heroes, but we don't love you that much. We are just going to cut these programs that help you." It's not right. Other veterans need these programs, not just myself. That's why these cuts have to stop. If we are your heroes, help us.

CAMILO MEJIA

National Guard Sergeant
Lives: Miami, Florida
Iraq War Service: March 2003–October 2003

When people hear me speak, they say, "How the hell did you wind up in the U.S. Army?"

Both my parents were very involved in the Sandinista Revolution in Nicaragua. My mother ran safe houses, and my dad was a musician, and at one point, he was considered the official musician of the revolution. He wrote the Sandinista hymn.

After the revolution, my mother worked for the Sandinista government. I lived in a very privileged position in Nicaragua. We didn't have a lot of capital, but we had a lot of influence. Then the Sandinistas lost the elections. My mother remained a public figure, though, but since the Sandinistas weren't in power, she was in pretty bad shape, and my parents were also separated. So we moved to Costa Rica, which is where she was from and where I had been born. I lived there for two years, and then my grandmother got my mother a green card, and we came to the States in 1994. I finished high school here in Miami. I went to public school and had to work to help pay rent and put food on the table.

I felt like I was not part of anything; I felt disconnected to the world. I worked at Burger King throughout high school, did sales, went into sales marketing. I did go to college but didn't feel ready for it. At the time, it seemed as though I needed a radical change. I needed to do whatever it took to be a part of society. Instead of becoming a political icon, like my parents, I decided to find my own path and find my own way. I joined the U.S. Army.

The army seemed like the best thing in the world. The recruiter told me the army was great, that you live in these college-like barracks, you'll have comrades, and you'll train with people and eat with people. It seemed so great. Finally, I could be part of something and make friends who'll last forever, have financial stability, not have to worry about bills. I'll get to travel and get to be an infantryman. I thought about war as a heroic thing you do for God and country. You fight for freedom, for democracy, to defend your home and loved ones, and so I joined in 1995.

My mom is not happy with me joining. But neither of my parents looked at it as "What have you done to my name?" It was more like, "Oh, my God. My kid is in the army."

For the most part I had a great experience in active duty. I was stationed in Fort Hood, Texas. I'm a mechanized infantryman. I did very well. I got an army commendation, a medal, an army reorganization medal, a service ribbon, a national defense ribbon, an army achievement medal, and a good conduct medal. I got out of active duty service in 1998. Every military contract is eight years long. My program was three and a half years. But whether you go National Guard or not, you still owe a total of eight years. So when I got out, I decided instead of doing eight years as a civilian, I would get into the National Guard. I finished community college, then got into the University of Miami.

In January 2003, about three months before the end of my military contract, one semester away from graduation, while I'm looking to get into graduate school, they tell us that we have been activated to participate in Operation Iraqi Freedom. All our contracts were extended.

We got activated January 15, and my service end date was May 21. That's when the war got more personal. I had never really thought about it much. I opposed it politically. I didn't really feel the government had made a case for war. The United Nations, France, Germany, China, Russia, even the Dixie Chicks were saying no war. So I questioned, but I didn't care a whole lot. I wanted my degree, I wanted to be a dad to my daughter, and I wanted to live a comfortable life. I kept thinking there may be no war, that we may just be scaring this guy out of power, and if there is, it will be quick and painless.

I went to Iraq, in part, because I was afraid to say no. I also think that very deep inside there was always this sense of wonder of what's it like in war. Soldiers are also so afraid to stand up to authority, but even more than that, it's your peers. A lot of soldiers tell you they disagree with the war, that it's for rich people, but we are also fighting for one another. Once you're there, it's a bond stronger than family. Your life depends on another person, and his life depends on you. You don't want your comrades to see you as a coward or a traitor.

We were deployed in March 2003. Our first mission was at a detention camp. The prisoners were on sleep deprivation for 48 hours. Here is how you keep them on sleep deprivation: You yell at them, and they are surrounded by wire that is much worse than barbed wire because instead of having points, it has blades, very sharp blades. Their hands are tied, and you yell at them. You tell them to "Get down, turn around, arms up and arms down, arms out." How do you get them to understand? Well, if you yell at them enough, they get it. If that doesn't work, you get this huge sledge hammer and hit the wall next to them, and it sounds like an explosion, and it scares the hell out of them. If that doesn't work, you get a pistol and cock it next to their ear and perform a mock execution. Every now and then, you let them sleep for 10 to 30 seconds. When they wake up, they don't know where they are or how long they have been asleep. I was a squad leader, so I didn't have to do it myself, but my men were doing it. I remember my platoon sergeant saying this doesn't meet Red Cross or Geneva Convention standards. There were no medical people around except the platoon's medic, and God knows how many other violations were found. He was thinking of calling the Red Cross, but he was told that if he did that, he would piss off the commander and mess up his career, and conditions for these people would not improve. So he didn't do anything, and neither did I.

Our next mission was securing a power plant where there had been some fierce fighting between the rangers and Republican Guard. The guard's men were buried there in shallow graves, only about 18 inches deep. The smell got so bad that the Iraqis told me wild dogs dog pulled them out and started eating them. The Iraqi people had to bury them somewhere else. There was a dam there. People who worked there just showed up, and they didn't get paid. They didn't have the parts needed to fix the place, but they would show up. I got to know them. They wanted to talk to you. We were welcomed at first because we got rid of Saddam, but they said it's time for us to go. They wanted to take control of their lives and country.

One time, they thought the insurgents may still be around after hours, and so they decide to send my squad and me near the place where there had been firefights. We were to set up a traffic control point and check cars. It's like midnight. Everyone has a really bad feeling about this. It's a dark place. They keep us there three hours. I was the squad leader and in charge. I'm riding with one team leader, and the other team leader is riding in the front humvee. Before we leave, I tell the drivers and team leaders, "Look, we are probably going to get ambushed because we've been here too long and especially because we are a small element and traveling a long distance, and there are only but so many routes you can take. Chances are, they are going to be waiting for us with an ambush." I told them, "Don't stop—just return fire," based on my military training. I know for a moving ambush the standard operating procedure is to return fire and get out of the area.

So we leave at three in the morning. I can see in front of the lead humvee that there is a box and then a wire attached to it. We are in this area where on both sides are buildings that have been bombarded by the war, skeleton buildings. I hear a whistle, and as we are coming around a curb, I say to myself, "Ambush." As I say it, the box in the middle of the road goes off. There is a big explosion, and it swallows up the humvee. And the humvees have gunners on top, and I see the gunner of the lead humvee just collapse into the hull, and the humvee almost comes to a halt. It slows down a lot. All of this happens in like a second or two, and then on the rooftops, I start seeing flashes from the barrels of guns and the sparks on the road from the bullets that are hitting the road. And all we have are flak vests, which are not really bulletproof. The vehicles we have had no armor, and, on top of that, they didn't have any doors. I'm thinking the guys in front of me are probably all dead. God only knows if the insurgents have rocket-propelled grenades, and they are shooting from the rooftops. I am watching all this in a kind of a trance. Part of me was ready for it, but at the same time I'm having a really difficult time digesting it. The guy in my humvee starts fighting, and that sort of wakes me up. I snap out of it, and I just start shooting into the darkness.

This whole time I'm not afraid. It's so surreal. Then I look forward and see the gunner of the other vehicle has come back up, and the humvee starts to pick up speed. The guys are not dead, and then we pick up speed. I'm so happy and excited that they are alive and that we might make it. So we get out of the kill zone and haul ass back to base. We get out of our humvees and start celebrating: "Yeah, we made it. The motherfuckers didn't kill us."

It was a concussion bomb, and it had no shrapnel in it. The blast temporarily blinded the driver, which is why he slowed down. So while we are celebrating, the commander, first sergeant, and executive officer call me upstairs with my two team leaders to brief them on what just happened, and I told them. The insurgents had a bomb and had people shooting at us for a span of about three blocks. They had the advantage. They were shooting down at us. God only knows what else they had if we didn't get out of there. I followed procedure. They were like, "Why didn't you stay and fight?" I said I followed standard operating procedure for a moving ambush. We returned fire and moved out of the kill zone. They all started talking, saying that they were glad that we were OK and that they understood the procedure, but that we sent the wrong message to the enemy. That we showed them we were afraid and not willing to fight, and now they are probably feeling victorious because we got away and didn't stay there and fight. They said we should have fought and called in backup. But backup would have taken 30 to 45 minutes to get there. At the squad level, a 45-minute firefight has the potential to kill every single soldier.

In Vietnam or World War II, a 45-minute firefight is nothing. But in this kind of urban warfare, it would have been a helluva firefight and would have killed every single one of us. We did not have armored humvees. It would have been a violation of army procedure to have stayed there and fight. So I kept my position, and they kept saying they understood, but we should have stayed. So at this point I stopped arguing. These are my superior officers. I'm wasting my time, wasting my saliva with these people. For me, it's a victory because my entire squad is untouched after an ambush. I had been in the military for eight years. Surviving an ambush is very unlikely, and I was really happy that we all made it out.

When I left that room, I felt like we had another enemy to worry about. Not just the insurgents and the bombs on the road and the RPGs [rocket-propelled grenades] but our own leadership. It didn't seem like there was a concern about the safety and well-being of the soldiers. There was more concern about sending a message, even if it means breaking procedure or killing soldiers and civilians. They don't care. They just want to kill people and capture people because it looks good on their records, and that's how you get medals.

The next day my platoon leader comes up to me and said he talked to my commander about what happened. He said, "It seems as though when you guys came back, you were celebrating that you had gotten away. I'm supposed to tell you that you are not supposed to do that because not only are you sending the wrong message to the enemy, but also, you are sending the wrong message to other soldiers in the unit by celebrating that you escaped when you should have stayed. It tells everyone it's OK to get away."

I couldn't believe my platoon leader was telling me this. Now this is someone who lives with the platoon, who goes out and fights, and he is telling me don't celebrate the fact that no one got killed. From then on, it was like everything we were trained to do, we did the exact opposite. As an infantryman, they train you to follow different routes, not to do the same mission the same exact way every day. To not stay at one place too long. By Geneva Convention standards, you are not supposed to conduct missions near hospitals, mosques, schools, or residential areas. We broke every rule there was.

We had a mission of traffic control stop right near their biggest mosque in Armani. We stopped traffic completely. What you were supposed to do was ask them to get out of the car, pat them down, and search the car. If nothing is there, you let them go. But the way my platoon leader was doing it was that he was searching people and then putting them next to a wall by the mosque, and he had an extra team of soldiers drive the car, like a valet, to another area. Then we'd detain the people for another hour. We are doing this by a mosque, and we are detaining people, and we are driving their cars, all which we are not supposed to do. People who were doing nothing wrong are being detained, and we were staying there too long.

After a while this car comes down, and they ordered him to stop so he could be searched. For some reason he does not stop. And they open fire on this guy. I remember I was standing between two trucks talking to another guy, and I see this car rolling at a very low speed. Ever hear the expression "We lit him up"? Well, this car was literally lit up by the amount of bullets that were actually penetrating the metal, the amount of sparks. It takes a lot of fire to hit metal, to actually light it up. My first response was to shoot at it, and I started shooting at this vehicle, but this guy is completely dead. His head is hanging from a fraction of what used to be his neck, and the vehicle is completely bullet ridden. I see that these soldiers are still firing, and I'm like, "What the hell are they still shooting at?" I now look up at the rooftop and see that there are now people shooting down at us because we started shooting at this guy who wouldn't stop, because he probably had brake trouble or something. It triggered an attack from the insurgents. So they are shooting at us with AK-47 machine guns.

We then fire at them right there, with all those innocent people who were being detained. It was a 25-minute firefight that ended with seven dead civilians plus others who went to the hospital. God know how many of those died. Two soldiers were injured. No one even moved this man from in front of the mosque. He stayed until the next morning. I don't know if they did that by mistake or left him there to send a message. But these are one of these incidents that the soldiers didn't mean to kill the citizens, but the leadership does things in a way where you know civilians are going to get killed. This is what happens when you go out of your way to instigate firefights.

I lost count of how many times we did raids. They were really dumb. Most of the successful raids we had were random. We were doing patrols, and we saw someone suspicious, and they saw us and ran, and then we'd search the neighborhood and find weapons, bomb-making equipment, anti-Coalition material, and things like that. But most of the organized raids were based on flawed intelligence. One time we went and raided this real upper-class neighborhood. We were looking for this guy like really high official of the Baath Party [Hussein's political party]. They said he was about 5'7", dark hair and dark skin, and he looks Iraqi. It sounds stupid, but we went looking for this guy based on that information. No one could pronounce his name, you know what I'm saying, so you go and raid this entire freaking neighborhood on this type of information,

One time, we had this house raid. They used two or three platoons for it. We went into these two brothers' houses at like 3 A.M. in the morning. They lived next door to each other. One was supposed to be making road bombs; the other was supposed to be storing them at his house. Turns out the person who gave us the information, the informer, was the cousin of the brothers, and there was a family feud. The cousin was pissed off at the brothers, so he figured he'd get the Americans to raid their house. We found nothing.

We would do raids in the houses, and sometimes the women and the kids would cry. It was pretty bad. We'd call them names. You don't do these things because you are evil. You don't call people hadji[1] because you are racist and look down on people because they are Arab or Muslim. You do it because it's a way to escape not just physical injury but moral and spiritual injury, because when you oppress them, and you treat them like shit and put a gun to their head in their own house in front of their family at three in the morning, it's a lot easier when you don't treat them like human beings and when you call them names. It's a process of dehumanization.

It was really hard on my unit. With the National Guard, a lot of people have businesses, jobs, or are going to school. They have families, or just got married, or have families not used to long deployments. There was a lot of hardships there. People's relatives were dying. A lot of us had prior active duty or were kids in college who joined for the tuition. In my case, I have been the military eight and a half years. I should not have been stop-loss.[2] I should not have been sent to Iraq. I am not a citizen, and when you are not a citizen, you can't be extended past the eight-year contract. As a Costa Rican citizen, there is a treaty that the country cannot force citizens into military service.

They violated the treaty and army regulations, plus my green card was expiring. So I wrote a letter to the commander saying my green card was expiring, that I'm not supposed to be here, didn't want to be here, and he should send me home to take care of this. He was like, "I don't know, because we are at war, and I want to do anything I can do to keep you here." But he then he decided to send me home for two weeks to fix the residency problem, and he sent the people who had hardship home for two-week leaves.

---

[1]"Hadji" is a Muslim teenage character in the syndicated cartoon series *Jonny Quest*.
[2]A military policy that may extend a tour of duty during wartime.

© AP Photo/U.S. Army, Pfc Benjamin Brody

I come home and try to find people to help me with this situation. I get told I should never have been deployed, but your commander had unlimited power and you have to go back. They told my attorney there was a computer glitch, and they thought I was a citizen.

I didn't really know I wasn't going back until I didn't go back. It was the most difficult and painful decision I ever made in my life. I remember the day I was supposed to go on the plane. I just slept through, and you think, "Maybe the next day I'll get on that plane." It was a hurricane of emotions and doubts. My attorney told me the president has unlimited power to do what he wants to do. He said we couldn't use a civilian judge, and most likely they were going to slam me, but I had a strong case. I stayed underground. So I went to New York and Boston and gave underground interviews.

On March 15, 2004, I surrendered. I gave a press conference and said I wasn't going to be part of the war and then surrendered myself. I was confined to the base for two months, tried, and sentenced to 12 months. I lost two-thirds of my pay and was dishonorably discharged. In a way I was surprised. We knew we had a very powerful case legally, but by going public I challenged the government. They didn't want to hear the witnesses, struck down the motions we had, and sentenced me.

I served my time in Fort Sill, Oklahoma. I got out in nine months for good behavior. After dealing with combat, jail seemed like therapy, like a resort. You had ice cream and cappuccino machines, coffee machines, and soda machines. In Iraq, we slept on cots and sleeping bags.

When I went to jail, I felt liberated. I didn't feel a like a prisoner; I felt empowered. At first, the inmates treated me like a weird animal. I had been in the *New York Times* and *USA Today*, and people use to protest for me outside. They would call me "CNN." They felt like I was not one of them, but then I started making friends.

I don't regret what I did. When people say I'm a coward, I say I was a coward for not standing up in the first place and saying this war is wrong. I feel shame because I felt it was somebody else's problem. If I have any regrets, it's in not doing more. There's a reason for everything. Maybe God put war in my path so I could see its ugly face and tell its story.

TY SIMMONS

National Guard Chief Warrant Officer

Lives: Aurora, Illinois

Iraq War Service: March 2003–July 2004

I bleed red, white, and blue. To me there is no greater honor than fighting for your country. I love my country so much. It's the best country in the world, and I am so proud to be among the many people dating back to the Revolution, the Civil War, who have served. I was 19 when I served in the Vietnam War and 53 when I was in Iraq. I have served in the military for 36 years.

You have to take the politics out of it. Today, we are having a lot of controversy— and it seems to be increasing—about the Iraq War. But I can tell you this: when I was in Iraq, the young soldiers among me in my company, the great majority, just wanted to do their job. Soldiers are not politicians. We are there to do a job. True soldiers, the guys down and dirty in the ditches, can't second-guess what is right and wrong.

I enlisted to serve in 1968 and was in Vietnam for one year. At the time, there was a lot of protesting going on. I signed up for a combination of reasons. I wasn't sure what I wanted to do with my life. I was 18. My folks wanted me to go to college, but the bottom line is, I wasn't ready. The army seemed like fun even though there was a war going on. An 18-year-old doesn't think about death and dying. I always wanted to fly, and I became a helicopter pilot. It wasn't long after we were there that people were dying. But although it was happening around me, you went out every day and did your job. As 19-year-old aviators, we did a lot of smoking and drinking. After getting the shit scared out of you on a mission, you'd clean up your bird [helicopter], took a shower, went to the officers' club, and you drank. Those were the days of the continuous happy hour.

I spent six years in the active army and got out in 1974. Then I went into the National Guard a week after I got out of the army. I left the army to get my degree and make my parents happy finally.

I was called up for the first Gulf War. They called and said, "Ty, we are looking for pilots. You are one of the old-timers, and you are experienced. They are sending a medevac unit, and if you're interested, you can go in a couple of days." I had a wife and family, a job with the state police, but I was willing to go. They called me back a few days later and said, "You won't have to go to the Gulf. What you are going to do is go to Fort Hood, Texas, and augment an active army unit." I said I would not be willing to do that. I had no desire to go. If I was going to leave my family, I wanted to do something that was real—not that that wasn't real, but it wasn't like going to war and going overseas. So I did not go.

When the Iraq War started, I remember saying to my wife, "Well, I hope this time they call me, and it's not to go to Fort Hood." I was joking. Then I got the call one afternoon to report in 48 hours.

I was the old guy. The young kids called me "Pops." I can't tell you how many mothers and fathers I told, "I'll bring your boy back home." That was another responsibility I took upon myself, and, you know, the reality is, I don't have a lot to do with that. But when you tell a parent, you have to do what you need to do. All I could do was be a strong force. I had to be hard. I could never allow myself to break down in front of them.

I was part of a CH-47 helicopter company. We flew the largest helicopters, Chinooks, and they are used mostly for transport. We initially were based in Kuwait. We ran a shuttle where we took troops and supplies from Kuwait to points north in Iraq.

After the push into Iraq, we took up residency in Balad, about 40 miles north of Baghdad. We did transport and resupply missions for all the ground units. I was the unit's operations officer, which was not intended. I'm a warrant officer, and usually real officers do that job, but our captain got ill and came down with kidney stones. My commander came to me one evening when we were flying together, and he said, "How would you like to be my operations officer?" I said, "No. I'm just a pilot. I want to be out with the guys." You know, being an operations officer, you don't fly, and I wanted to be a pilot. He said that's where I was needed, and I would do the scheduling and could fly when I wanted to.

My assignment entailed not as much flying as I would have liked, but I would like to think I did a good job. We brought nearly everyone home, but my unit did suffer one of the first losses. We had a Chinook shot down back in September '03. Twenty-something people were killed, including three of our crewmembers.

It was sad, very traumatic. I was tested to my max, not because of the war environment but because of the young people around me. It was one of those days you'll never forget. We were in operations, and we heard there was a helicopter that had been shot down, and there was instant panic. Communications wasn't so great at that time, and they didn't say what type it was. Then we found out it was a Chinook, we kept checking and narrowed it down that it was one of ours. Then we got the tragic news. Lost the pilot and crewmembers from our brigade. I knew the crew who died. I lost a personal friend of 18 years.

In Vietnam, hearing people get shot down and killed was tough. But since I was in a position of authority like I was in Iraq, I became a focal point. People expected me to know what to do. I had to have the answers. I lived through death in Vietnam, but back then, I was just another pilot. Someone dies, we went to the club and got drunk. We toasted them and toasted them. In Iraq, I had to answer questions. I had to be responsible.

If they had pulled an aircraft up to our hangar the week after the Chinook went down and said, "Everyone who wants to go home, get on board," a large percentage of the soldiers would have got on and left. It was pretty traumatic. You had young people who never even lost a family member. They are young. Now they lost three people they broke bread with, knew, laughed with, and talked with. In Iraq, we all went together as a company. In Vietnam, other than the first units that went, soldiers were sent in as replacements. There were always the seasoned guys there. When we went to Iraq, we were it, the old and the new. It was traumatic and emotional and tough at times for me. It was painful trying to maintain the unit, to hold it together. My commander was younger than I am, so was my captain. I didn't cry in front of the soldiers. No one saw me cry, but my wife heard me cry. I couldn't show emotion in front of them. I was supposed to be the tough guy, the Vietnam vet, seasoned pilot, and senior operations officer. I had to be tough for the young kids. It's a role I had to take on. It would have been not good to get emotionally strung out. We were still in a war zone. We still had a job to do.

A lot of maturity took place after that. We took a lot of young people there and brought them back as mature adults. I just attended a wedding of two enlisted folks who met in Iraq. Then you have my friend who died, whose children will never see him again. That's what war is about. People die.

I have two kids, a son who is 24 and a 21-year-old daughter. I missed milestones in their lives. I missed my son's college soccer games and my daughter graduating from high school. I missed her

going off to college. She called me when she was moving into the dorm. She said, "Daddy, you won't believe it. It is so hot in here." I said, "How hot is it?" She said, "It's got to be 90 degrees." I said, "Oh, really. It's 120 here."

I was 53 when I was in Iraq. I felt sometimes like, "Oh, my God, what am I doing here?" On tough days, I thought about my family and what would they do without me. How would I get buried? Gosh, I thought I'd never seen my grandkids, never get to walk my daughter down the aisle. I never thought about those kinds of things in Vietnam. As a 53-year-old man, no matter how much I'd like to think I'm in good shape and physically fit, I'm wearing down. The old body ain't taking it. There are aches and pains. The God-awful heat and dust—it was hard, tough. I used to joke maybe if I could have a beer at night, I would have felt better the next day, but you couldn't have a beer. There was no booze in Iraq, which is a big difference from Vietnam. The military chose to make it booze-free out of respect for the Muslim faith. But there is booze all over the place, and the Iraqis try and sell it to you. There's also pornographic material, pinups, but you couldn't have any of that stuff. The military thought it would be degrading, and while I understand the philosophy behind it, they were all over. The Iraqis and Kuwaitis had the magazines, the porn. It was on satellite TV. It was raunchy, to put it bluntly. It's a joke, but it didn't matter. Those were the rules, whether you like it or not.

My unit was extended three times. Last time we were extended was almost as bad as dealing with the shootdown. The reason we got extended I understand. It was the right thing to do. We were the most experienced Chinook company in Iraq. The units before us had left, and new ones were coming in. From a military point of view, it was the right thing to do. There was an insurgency uprising going on. I took a long walk and cursed and kicked the stones when no one was around, because I could not allow myself to break down in front of the young soldiers. I think the way I acted may have hurt me. They thought I was cold and uncaring. I wanted to see my wife and my family, but it would not have done good for them to see me break down. I did a silent grieving. I was in Iraq for 15 months.

I did not really make up my mind to get out of the military until I'd been home a while. When I looked at my family's life for the 18 months I was gone and the pain we endured, I didn't want to put them through that again. We were empty nesting; my wife was by herself; her parents are two hours away. My wife was alone many nights, by herself like many other military wives. I decided that I didn't need to put my wife through that again even though she didn't complain. As much I like going off and playing war, I don't need to do that again. People wanted me to stay. There were a lot of emotional twist and turns, but I retired after 36 years.

I miss the flying, the camaraderie. I have been awarded the Silver Star, Distinguished Flying Cross, two Bronze Stars from Vietnam, and several air medals, but soldiers don't go to war to get medals.

If people can only understand what the war truly means to the majority of the Iraqi people, the freedom we are giving the Iraqi people. It's not talked about much. Our country was founded by the lives we lost. Whenever people die in a war, it's hard, but you have to stay the course and hope and pray. You've got to support the soldier. After Vietnam, I was a nobody. I was spat upon, discarded. I was called a baby killer. I hope and pray that we never do that again, that the young soldiers will not have to go through that. The soldiers are just doing their job, the best way that we can. Always support the soldier in the fight even if you may not like what the government is doing. You may not like why they are there, but please support the soldiers. The difference between you and a soldier is, you can walk into work and say, "I quit." You are not going to get arrested. You are not going to go to jail, but a young soldier can't say, "I quit." A soldier would get arrested—they would be AWOL, a criminal.

These young soldiers are heroes. We need to support them no matter what.

Acknowledgments

I want to say a heartfelt, enormous thank-you to the vets who let me in their homes, hospitals, heads, and hearts. I feel very lucky to live in a country where people like these men and women and countless others like them are so willing to stand up and defend us and our rights to be who we are. There is no way to fully comprehend their sacrifice. We could all say thank you every minute of every day, and it still would not be enough.

I want to thank all the folks at PoliPointPress but most especially my publisher, Scott Jordan, a Vietnam veteran who truly cares about vets and their stories; my editor, Peter Richardson, who was supportive, caring, and always seemed to say the right things; Carol Pott; Kim Shannon; copy editor Laura Larson; and one of my favorite people in the entire world, PoliPointPress marketing director Rhoda Dunn.

A lot of people and organizations helped me find the vets in this book, among them Sarah Ryan of the Army's Operation Tribute to Freedom; Matt Taylor of The Wounded Warrior Project; Operation Truth; Maj. Gregory Heilshorn of the New Hampshire National Guard; Iraq Veterans against the War; Dan Lohaus, director of the documentary on homeless veterans title *When I Came Home*; Lester Outterbridge, a Gulf War veteran and an amazing man; Daniel Sagalyn, and all the people who advocate on both political fronts for veterans.

I also want to thank Barbara Laker; Jenice Armstrong; Marisol Bello; L. A. Banks; Jack Morrison; Janet and Lenny Barag; Lisa Nelson Haynes and the Painted Bride Art Center; Anita Spector; Don and Jayne Spector; Nicole Kilcullen; Trish Wilson; Myung Oak Kim;

Scott Flander; Don Russell; Elmer Smith; Zack Stalberg; Michael Days; and all my buddies at the *Philadelphia Daily News*, but most especially the fabulous reporter and editor Val Russ, who read everything and helped me get this book together.

Thanks to my dealmaker, Lisa A. Davis of Frankfurt Kurnit Klein & Selz; my fantastic publicist, Simone Cooper; my very smart students at Villanova University; and Dr. John Huxford and Dr. Teresa Nance. I want to thank my mother, Ramona Latty; my uncle, Luis Germosen; and my godmothers, Grace Vincent and Beryl Carroll. They have all believed in me and encouraged me since I was a kid with big dreams.

Thank you to Shelley Spector for her endless support and courage in dealing with me when I was on deadline, overwhelmed, and emotional.

My cousin, Marine S.Sgt. Scott "Scottie" Germosen, a husband, father, and son, lost his life in a plane crash over Pakistan. He was one of the first soldiers killed in the war on terror. I learned of his death on the television news. Our families have long since lost touch. In many ways my memory of playing with Scottie, then a little dark-haired boy, inspired this book. May he rest in peace.

ABOUT THE AUTHOR

YVONNE LATTY is a former reporter for the *Philadelphia Daily News* and teaches journalism at Villanova University. She is the author of *We Were There: Voices of African American Veterans, from World War II to the War in Iraq*. She lives with her family in Philadelphia, Pennsylvania. You can visit Yvonne at www.yvonnelatty.com.